Fruit Trees

Simple Steps to Abundant Fruit Production

(Start Your Fruit Trees Garden in Even the Smallest Backyard)

Frank Howerton

Published By **Ryan Princeton**

Frank Howerton

Fruit Trees: Simple Steps to Abundant Fruit Production (Start Your Fruit Trees Garden in Even the Smallest Backyard)

ISBN 978-1-9994868-6-0

No part of this guidebook shall be reproduced in any form without permission in writing from the publisher except in the case of brief quotations embodied in critical articles or reviews.

Legal & Disclaimer

The information contained in this book is not designed to replace or take the place of any form of medicine or professional medical advice. The information in this book has been provided for educational & entertainment purposes only.

The information contained in this book has been compiled from sources deemed reliable, and it is accurate to the best of the Author's knowledge; however, the Author cannot guarantee its accuracy and validity and cannot be held liable for any errors or omissions. Changes are periodically made to this book. You must consult your doctor or get professional medical advice before using any of the suggested remedies, techniques, or information in this book.

Upon using the information contained in this book, you agree to hold harmless the Author from and against any damages, costs, and expenses, including any legal fees potentially resulting from the application of any of the information provided by this guide. This disclaimer applies to any damages or injury caused by the use and application, whether directly or indirectly, of any advice or information presented, whether for breach of contract, tort, negligence, personal injury, criminal intent, or under any other cause of action.

You agree to accept all risks of using the information presented inside this book. You need to consult a professional medical practitioner in order to ensure you are both able and healthy enough to participate in this program.

Table Of Contents

Chapter 1: How to Choose, Plant and Care for Fruit Trees

What's better than fresh harvested apple or peach straight from the tree? Do you like a fresh apple pie that's made from apple slices you've taken yourself from the window of your kitchen? If you're not sure what a delicious and delicious apple directly from the trees is in comparison to the ones you get at the local supermarket shop, (Or worse... canned in a factory!) it might be worth considering making yourself a fruit trees!

A few people already have the pleasure of the gardening of vegetables or flower and fruit-based gardening. However, it could be that plantation can seem a bit difficult for someone who has had no experience with arboreal gardening. Don't worry! By doing a little investigation, establishing fruit trees is the perfect way to earn profits that are sweet. They are an excellent investment because, it is not just possible to harvest and consume them when they are in season, but there are plenty of ways of storing and using for the rest of the year! This article is to provide you with an idea of what that you require to begin in the process of planting and harvesting your fruits of your choice.

Choosing the Right Trees

Be aware of the Cold-Hardiness Zone

The initial step for making sure that the tree you plant will produce the best fruit is knowing the zone of cold-hardiness. The term "hardiness zone" is an area that is geographically identified that a certain category of plants is able to grow in accordance with the climate as well as its capability to stand up to the hottest temperatures within the zone. The cold hardiness zones are an effective tool for determining which plants are best suited to thrive outdoors in specific regions, but it's an only tool that you make use of when deciding which varieties can thrive in the particular climate of your. The drawback to having a zone for hardiness without other studies is that it doesn't include information on the summer temperatures. A few areas that are part of the zone of hardiness (thus with the same or comparable winter weather conditions) could have drastically different summer weather conditions in terms of as temperature or rainfall. This could be detrimental for trees in the event that you aren't getting enough rain, or your summers aren't cool enough or too humid in other trees suitable for the region you live in.

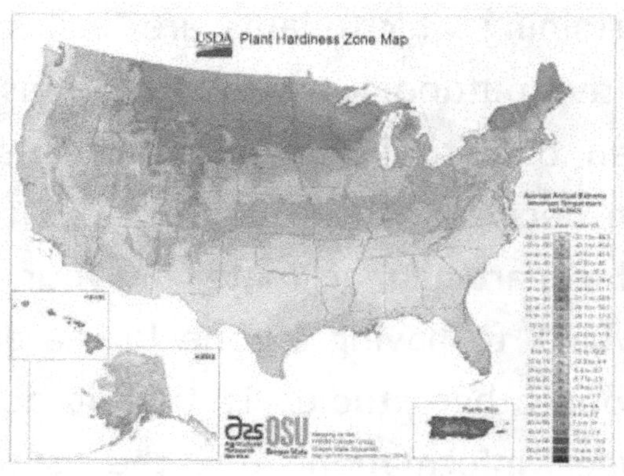

Zones and Climate

Certain kinds of trees thrive most effectively in cold winters (certain apple varieties, pears or cherries) Some thrive in warm, sunny environments (especially citrus) however, the majority thrive in mild climate that has warm temperatures in the summer and moderate winters. It is a good idea to search for varieties which are native to the region in which you reside. They have adapted to the seasons, temperature and the conditions that you need to contend with and are able to thrive with lesser effort than the other types of trees. One disadvantage is that it can restrict your options; both sizes of trees and varieties of fruit that are grown. (For instance, if you are in the wet Northwest or in the winter cold in the Northeast it is likely that citrus fruits would prove to be a greater problem to cultivate as opposed to a place similar to California and Florida).

Other elements that impact the survival of plants include winter snow cover stability and soil moisture levels and humidity, as well as the amount of frost days, as well as the chance of an extreme freezing storm. If, for instance, you reside in a region with a regular winter snowfall, it will give you better-than-average tree traits. If the snowfall in your locality is sporadic or intermittent, it is something you'll be able to think about when picking trees.

Certain trees aren't able to do well in extreme wet weather (peaches for instance) and thrive in dry and warm zones (like Georgia) but can thrive in other locations so long as the summer's growing season is sufficiently long and dry.

Certain species also need certain circumstances that impact the way they flower and fruit including day length as well as vernalization (some plants require a time of lower temperatures to signify that they are in flower or about to fruit). Consult a local tree nursery for advice on trees will help you gain a better understanding of what you can expect for your region.

In spite of your location you must choose at least two trees which have pollinators that are compatible to create the best set of fruits. It is crucial to pair trees because the trees require the capability to cross-pollinate in order in order to produce fruits! The late and mid-season apples typically taste better and are more durable to store than the early season varieties. If you're able to get the space and desire a more prolonged harvest selecting both later and early season varieties can yield apples in late summer/early autumn (August) until October There are some varieties that can produce more late in autumn/winter (like "Opal," which is which is a yellow-colored apple).

Basic Types of Fruit Trees

Pome Fruits

The apples and the pears are referred to as pome fruits. They are part of the family of plants known as Rosaceae. They have the "core" comprised of a few tiny seeds that are surrounded by a tough membrane. The membrane is enclosed in an edible flesh layer. There are around 7,500 distinct varieties of apple cultivars and around three thousand different cultivars of peaches Each one is well-suited to various climates, seasons and harvest time, as well as the soil and requirements for space.

Apples are among the most sought-after tree fruit due to their adaptable, fairly simple to cultivate and offer numerous applications. The optimal pH of soil for apples is neutral or very slightly acidic around 6.5 However, apple trees are able to adapt to acidic soils if the soil is healthy and well-drained. A majority of varieties of apples are adaptable to cold-hardiness zones 4 to 7. However, you'll require low-chill varieties like "Anna" or "Pink Lady' for milder winter temperatures.

Apples that are ripe in the early seasons mature first and taste best when eaten as applesauce or Apples (like "Vista Bella" or the 'Gingergold' variety). September is the month when all the magical happens, and you will are able to enjoy the majority of the apple varieties ripening. It is a month that has some of the top and most well-known varieties that are commonly available in grocery stores. "Honeycrisp" and "Gala" are ripe around the middle of September. The 'McIntosh' apple also ripens around the middle of September. They are most tart and crunchy. In October, baking apples are available (like the 'Granny Smith' and Ida Red). They are the perfect apple for tarts and crispy crisps. If you're an apple-loving sweet fan"Fuji" is a popular choice at this time of the year and tastes as sweet as a Gala. There are several options that appear later however it is best to gather late-season (October) apple and preserve in the freezer for future use.

Apple trees are an excellent starting point because they're incredibly beautiful and easy to learn for novices. there are a myriad of applications in the kitchen, from drinks such as cider and juice (and when you add a bit of fermentation a truly beneficial and delicious vinegar) and applesauce to apple pie as well as crumble cakes, apple chips.

Pears may be less hardy to cold than apples, but they are more able to sustainably grow throughout a range of climates. Pears originate from the coastal regions and areas that are mildly temperate and can be found in the regions in North Africa and across Asia. Since antiquity, people were able to cultivate the pears in warmer climates too.

There are early and late season pear varieties (known as winter and autumn pear) they are both great for cooking and eating. What makes them different from the harvest time is the long-lasting the storage. "Bartlett" is one of the most famous varieties of pears, and the variety you will find the most at the grocery store. In zones 4 to 7 select varieties which are resistant to blight caused by fire for example "Moonglow" or "Honeysweet.. For Zones 5-8, Asian pear trees often produce gorgeous, crisp-fleshed fruit provided they are they are given routine maintenance.

Stone Fruits

The stone fruit is called a drupe. It is a fleshy outer layer that is enclosed by an outer shell (also known as the pit or the'stone') which protects the seed within. Certain stone fruits can be classified as'freestone in which the pit can be easily removed while clingstone is in which the pit is more durable. Most commonly, the trees grown for cultivation that produce stone/cling fruits include sweet and sour cherries nectarines, apricots and plums.

Cherries vary in color, ranging that ranges from bright yellow to black, and can be classified into two types: sweet varieties that include "Bing," or "Stella," as well as sour or pie cherries such as "Nanking," or "Montmorency". They have a short period of growth, and usually have their highest point in June or July. They're well adapted for zones 4-7 and are able to grow at all temperatures that are temperate.

Cherry trees require fertile, close to neutral soils as well as a good air circulation. The cultivation of 12-foot tall dwarf cherry trees in either type will make the protection of your crops from disease as well as birds. The smaller trees can be surrounded with nets of protection or sprays with sulfur or Kaolin clay. Birds love cherries! The typical cherry tree matures in the shortest amount of time If you don't pay to the time, birds can eat all of the cherries you harvest before even realizing that they're ready. The reason why you should net your the cherry trees has a major benefit.

Apricots are an exquisite deep yellow, with a soft, firm but delicious flesh with a distinct flavor. The first time they were cultivated, they were in areas similar to Armenia and Persia the preserved and dried fruit was extremely important and abundant along trade routes to be food items. The fruit was introduced into North America in the 17th century. But the bulk of the cultivars that are now grown of Apricots are derived from Spanish missionaries. Apricots are best suited to an area with chilly winters. However they are also able to grow in other kinds of climates when the winter is too cold for adequate sleep. Apricots like slightly dry conditions and are colder robust than the peaches.

Be aware that they bloom late in the year and a prolonged frost isn't good for an Apricot season. Apricots are prone to fungal and bacterial diseases such as a variety of rots and cankers, and mildew. Therefore, it's essential to be aware of the trees you plant to prevent the risk of outbreaks of disease before they become too out of hand. Important to know is that certain cultivars have self-compatible varieties (that is, they don't require pollinators trees) however this isn't all the time, so make sure you be sure to know what the prerequisites are for the specific kind you select.

Nectarines and peaches require an ideal site, prevention of pests and a bit of luck. Much more than the other varieties of fruit trees, peach and nectarine trees require an arid soil that is not soil that is compacted or hardpan. The nectarines and peaches are better adaptable to zones 5-8, however specific varieties can also be planted in warmer and colder environments.

Peach and nectarine tree species typically live for a short time due to wood-boring insects. Additionally, they are vulnerable to the blight that is due to cedar trees therefore, if you are planning to plant nectarine or peach trees, ensure that your location is far enough from the cedar tree. (For further information on the bugs and diseases, check later in the article)

The plums come in a variety of stonefruit, featuring soft or firm flesh that ranges from small and tart to huge and extremely sweet, and every combinations of the two. Also, they range in color with a variety of gold hues, including bright yellow and green to a reddish-purple and even a dark purple nearly black-blue. They can be dried well (prunes) and are stored as jellies and jams very effectively. The cultivation of the plum is practiced throughout history, with areas that span from the extreme east Asia up into eastern Europe and the Caucasus Mountains. The plum is currently in an area that extends to Western Europe and all across North America as well.

They tend to grow fruits in a random manner because trees usually lose their fruit due due to late freezes or diseases. If they're in good times, trees that grow plums will produce large harvests of delicious fruits with a range of colors between light green and deep purple. The best suited to zones 4-8, plum trees require at least one variety that is compatible nearby for the best pollination. The plums don't like particularly dry climates (they may not bear grow fruit) however, they may have problems if conditions are too humid (brown decay).

Citrus Fruits

Citrus is a term used in the common sense and Genus (Citrus) of flowersing plants of the rue family of Rutaceae. The cultivation of citrus fruit has occurred across a vast area from the beginning of time; and has expanded more and further thanks to new cultivation techniques (like the greenhousing). Prior to the widespread availability of long-distance transportation possibilities for fruit were made available and colder climates were more common, citrus was considered to be an exotic and exclusive food item. If you've ever thought about what the connection between citrus and Christmas, this tradition was born when the cost of oranges was high and scarce to obtain. They were used as Christmas gifts for stockings, and could even be the sole time throughout the year when people could get an orange.

The most famous examples of citrus include citrus fruits like oranges (both mandarin as well as navel) as well as limes, lemons as well as grapefruit and tangerines. Some lesser-known cultivars are Kumquat, Satsuma and the 'Meyer' variety of lemon. They are the most simple fruits trees to cultivate organically, in zones 8b through 10.

The oils that are present in the rinds and leaves of citrus provide the natural shield against bugs, but their cold-tolerance is a bit limited. Certain varieties of citrus trees might require the use of blankets if temperatures drop to below freezing. But fruit harvests in winter from homegrown citrus fruit will definitely be worth the effort. One other option for growing citrus in colder conditions is to plant them in the greenhouses in large sizes.

Growing in a greenhouse (also called hot-house or solarium growth) can be a fantastic option to extend the growing season or include species of plants or trees typically don't have the conditions for. The most affluent European estates (going to the 17th century in some instances) could include an orangery. This was a greenhouse/solarium specifically designed for the purpose of growing citrus in an ideal conditions. Glass (or contemporary polycarbonate) is used to create the walls and roofs greenhouses mimic the subtropical climate which citrus plants require to flourish.

The typical temperatures of greenhouses are maintained between 55 to 95 degrees Fahrenheit. They also experience some moisture. When the summer heat is on, it might be required to shade a portion of the structure in order to keep temperature rises However, this is achieved with a shade fabric or shutter screens that are pre-installed. If you notice that your greenhouse does not receive enough winter lighting, then adding lighting for growing could be helpful for encouraging trees to grow.

Certain varieties of citrus are also planted in containers, which will make the tree less invasive as well as having a large pot helps keep the tree in balance as it gets bigger and becomes top weighty. Take care! Although container-grown trees are less tinier than those that are planted conventionally but the trees along with the soil and the container will be extremely weighty! It is difficult for them to transport without the right equipment, so be sure to place your trees on a location that you are comfortable with, even if you've got a hand truck accessible. A second consideration with container-grown citrus is the condition in the soil. It is recommended to choose the right mix made for plants with a hot climate (like citrus or Cactus) and if you prefer to make your own mix, ensure that it drains properly. Cactus trees do not thrive when they have extremely moist roots. In order to aid in drainage of the container You can place pebbles on the bottom of your container. However, you shouldn't submerge your fruit! In the winter, or dormant time it is recommended to water them every week. In the summer months, it is recommended to water the tree every daily. If your leaves curl this is a sign the tree requires extra water.

When you are growing in a greenhouse or a container be sure to be attentive to soil health nutrition, drainage, and irrigation, since you are more room to make mistakes with closed areas. This will be discussed more in detail in the post following.

If you're growing your greenhouse in a container be sure to take special care of the quality of your soil nutrition, drainage, and watering as there is much less space for error in closed areas. This will be discussed thoroughly in the piece following.

Tree Sizes: Standard, Semi-dwarf, Dwarf

Fruits like pears, apples, and citrus offer a wide range of options in terms of the growth of trees is concerned, and range from the full-standard (standing at around 20 feet tall and wide) as well as semi-standard (about 75-90 percent of the standard size) as well as semi-dwarf (usually between 40 and 70% of the standard) and even the tiniest sizes of dwarfs, which typically are 25% of the normal size. When it comes to greenhouses the dwarf tree is almost always the most suitable choice since they don't grow in the same height or width as some other types of trees.

There aren't many choices for tree-sized rootstocks as they are all planted on normal roots. The exception is cherries. this as they have many semi-standard as well as semi-dwarf varieties. This issue can be cured through proper pruning and cultivation. This can limit tree size and spreading so that they are more manageable.

A semi-dwarf plant is an excellent alternative due to the balanced ratio of size controlability and toughness. It is more accommodating in the event of a few mistakes in the process of cultivating. Semi-dwarf fruit trees tend be well-anchored, and also have larger areas for fruit production, in comparison with dwarf fruit trees and all of this without taking up larger area.

Chapter 2: Rootstock and Graft Unions

The tree you're developing from is vital. "Rootstock" refers to the subterranean part of the plant (the root system itself) as well as the initial couple of inches which protrude out of the ground, to form the graft union. "The graft union" is the area where healthy roots the one tree is grafted to a cutting or bud of a different plant. The rootstock selected is chosen based on its interactions with the soil, its durability as well as its health. The graft that is placed on the rootstock is chosen because of its growth pattern and the characteristics of fruit bearing. The graft is visible in the middle of the tree. the trunk shows the slightest bend or bulge.

Selecting a reliable nursery to purchase your tree to purchase will affect the whole lifespan of your tree. The fundamental anatomy of a fruit tree includes the tree, a tree's graft union, and its root. The graft union is a tiny bump in the rootstock that is where two types of trees were joined for the creation of the tree. After a graft is made, it will take a few weeks to allow tissues from the two regions to join to form a single tree. Sometimes, in order to achieve the desired outcome it is the case that an entirely different species of tree was grafted to the desired variety to alter its traits (this occurs with apples as an example. Sometimes, they are grafted with quinces to create less sized trees).

If the grafting process isn't completed correctly, it can create a range of issues such as a different size tree from what is expected, the weak trunks, or an eventual split of the graft once the tree has expanded some and established it.

Optimum Growing Conditions

Fruit trees require full sunlight for their growth. The majority also need an adequately drained soil. However, the pears, apples and plums tend to be more than tolerant of conditions that aren't ideal. If you're experiencing drainage problems that are significant issue, then put your trees on raised beds.

Pick a spot that has the direct light of sunlight throughout the day for maximum results in fruit set. Avoid planting in shaded areas which don't receive at least a half-day of direct, full sunlight or you will anticipate weak, spindly plants with poor growth, low foliage as well as a poor set of fruit. Leave enough space between the plants and structures or trees and power lines, or any other obstacles to permit the trees to take up the space once it is fully grown. In order to cross-pollinate trees, plant them at least 50 feet from each other but between 15 and 20 feet in order to permit proper airflow and drainage.

Choosing and Preparing Your Site

Equally important to choosing the right tree to suit your climate and geographic location, planning the place for your trees is something you should carefully take into consideration. If you're an orchardist in your backyard, you might have a restricted space to plant your trees. Therefore, it is important to plan your trees carefully. If you have a small area the semi-dwarf or dwarf trees could be the ideal choice as they're the smallest footprint and the shortest reach. Additionally, it is possible to plant them further to each other than conventional trees. A few dwarf varieties can also work quite well in containers when you're not having enough ground space. Numerous factors on the location determine how trees can thrive, which includes drainage, soil composition sun hours, as well as wind exposure. It isn't a good idea to pick the most beautiful trees and then see them constantly suffocated by winds or buried in the soil.

Soil Composition

If you are able to think ahead making sure your soil is prepared over a period of time makes perfect conditions. It is possible to control the quantity of organic matter you can add by including compost, lawn clippings, debris like fallen leaves or the cover plant (like the red clover) in order to enrich the soil. If you can refrain from tilling the soil it will increase the number of beneficial organisms such as earthworms. Worms are great for the orchard as they produce healthy, well-aerated and mixed soils that are rich in nutrients. If you do not have the time or resources to set up your property in advance, it is possible to make use of potting soil that has been pre-mixed to fill in the holes and help your trees grow as they settle into their new habitat.

Hole Size and Depth

The hole you choose for your fruit tree must be two times the size of your root system as well as 2 feet in depth. The hole should be large enough to allow the roots to be covered completely. Avoid planting too deep because the tree could develop poorly. The graft joint should be exposed, and it must extend above the soil's line of 3 inches.

This is crucially important when dealing with smaller species. If the plant is in a way that is too deep, and the graft union lies beneath the soil line the scion (what you graft the rootstock to and the fruit you expect to get) grows roots, which will eventually turn into the size of a normal-sized tree.

If you are digging your hole, make sure to keep from glaring the sides of your hole (sides which are smooth and undamaged). This hinders the drainage process and can hinder root growth. One of the easiest ways to stop this is to use hand rakes or cultivators to tear the wall of the hole in order to create rough uneven.

Drainage Considerations

The majority of fruit trees cannot thrive in soil that drains in such a way that it is water saturated over long time. Roots of trees that are in a state of constant water saturation can prevent tree root system from being able exchange nutrients. They will then get waterlogged, and then begin to turn brown. The rot in the roots suffocates the tree. It starts to look ill as it loses leaves and becomes dry or weak. To prevent this from happening prior to planting, ensure that you know the drainage capacity of your soil.

For a test of drainage in your soil to determine the drainage of your soil, make a trench about one foot deep. Fill the hole with water. If it drains in three or four hours, then fill the hole with water again. If it takes more than three or four hours for the water to go away following the initial or second filling, then your soil does not drain properly enough for planting in, and you'll require a different spot, or do something to increase the aeration and drainage of the site. This could be accomplished by or using raised beds (although it isn't practical for trees that produce fruit) as well as using soil lightening agents on your soil. This could include organic matter (such as compost, leaves yard waste, manure for instance.) sandy loam (a soft and fluffy soil filler) soil) or porous substances such as perlite or pumice. If your soil is primarily clay, then you may also mix in Gypsum (calcium Sulfate) for helping to bind clay particles in order to expand micropores in soil.

If the soil drains properly however your property is receiving more water flowing through the other parts of your property, don't panic! The construction of swales, berms or dry streambeds for redirecting water could also aid in reducing the problem of moisture. Swales are an area that's low and intended to hold water and drain it out of other places. Berms are a flat area or a raised wall that divides two places (like the fruit trees you have from the water swale). Dry streambeds are less sloped surface, which is typically composed of rocks, stones and pebbles which funnel water away during rainy weather. There are numerous ways to limit the flow of water and divert it away. Consult the local garden center for assistance with drainage problems as well as check out a few self-help books available at the library for further information regarding how to create the perfect solution for your property.

Planting and Care

How To Plant

The ideal time to plant trees located in the zones 3-7 is the beginning of spring after the soil has been thawed. The fruit trees planted when they are emerging from winter dormancy can quickly establish new roots. For Zones 8-10 Plant new trees during February. Pick a site with a sunny location with well-drained, fertile soil that isn't within a low frost area. Create a trench (making sure that it's large enough and deep enough) and then spread the roots inside the hole. Then, back fill with soil. Plant the trees in the same level as they were growing in the nursery. Take careful not to submerge the Graft union (the knotted or bent region) located on the main trunk. Then, water the tree well, and put the trunk guard, made from material such as spiral or hardware cloth on the bottom of the tree to guard the tree from rodents, insects scorching sun and injury (more about this on this in section "Pests and Diseases" section further down). Take the tree down loosely in order to ensure it stays in place. The root zone should be covered with mulch. of the tree that is planted using sawdust, wood chips or any other slower-rotting mulch. Be sure to water well in dry periods during the initial two years. (Refer to the "Mulching" as well as "Watering" sections further down for additional details.)

Watering

When the tree is established and the hole is drained and the hole is filled, water your tree immediately with 3-5 gallons water. This will help to soak the soil. Make sure you do it in a slow manner so to ensure that water doesn't flow away or wash the soil away. When the water is absorbed, and the soil re-sets check that the graft joint remains at least 2 inches above the soil's level. If not, make adjustments according to the need.

The trees that are newly planted should be watered when the upper 2 inches of soil remain dry. If the rainfall level isn't sufficient (less than 1 inch every week) provide 3-5 gallons of water to the newly-planted trees every week in the beginning of the year of their growth. When the trees develop bigger roots, you will be able to reduce the frequency of watering, but be aware that for a fruit that is juicy the fruit trees should get a regular soaking (provided either by rainfall or through you). A proper watering schedule is crucial to ensure the condition of the tree and in addition, its quality crop. Water that is adequate creates the most delicious fruits. If you don't water properly the fruit that is produced is smaller, dry and bitter. The tree isn't going to flourish.

Drip systems work well for the cultivation of fruit trees. The drip system is an automated system for watering that is made up of hoses that have tiny holes drilled all over. If water is pumped through the hoses flows out of the holes slowly, and over a long period of time that allows it to be gently and completely deliver water to the roots. The majority of drip systems has a timer to ensure that trees are regularly watered. Even the simplest versions of drip systems are manually operated (turn the hose on and then switch off the hose) However, no matter what method you've set up you should check your trees on a regular basis to be sure they're being watered. Monitoring your hose lines is essential, as it will make certain that there are no cracks, kinks, splits or obstructions.

Mulching

Mulching can help conserve moisture in soil. The impact of mulch on soil moisture is quite complex. The mulch layer is a buffer in between the soil air that blocks evaporation from the surface, by forming barriers between the moist soil and dry air. It also hinders sunlight from reaching the soil's the surface. But, it can hinder water from entering the soil through absorbing or blocking gentle rain (this is a possibility to overcome with an underground drip system that is buried that is placed between soil and the the mulch layer). Mulch can also help to keep soil temperature from fluctuating excessively (this assists in winter when the roots are warmer). Mulch helps to keep the growth of weeds down, too, since it's more difficult for weeds and weeds to survive on the thick soil. The mulch layers typically are at least 2 inches in depth when they are applied. Additionally, when the mulch is broken down during the season, it provides nutrients to soil.

Mulch is made of diverse elements like sawdust, bark compost, manure, and yard waste (like grass clippings). There are organic forms of mulch, too (including sheets of plastic and shredded rubber) however they can alter the pH balance and chemical composition of the soil. They also risk not breaking down in the soil with time.

Fertilizing

They require several elements to grow, such as the sun, airflow and water. Additionally, they require substances from soil. They are the primary macro-nutrients, which include nitrogen, phosphorus, as well as potassium. Secondary nutrients are calcium, magnesium and sulfur. There are also micronutrients which include iron, zinc manganese, copper molybdenum, boron and chlorine. Each of them plays an important function in promoting the growth of plants and in the event that any of them is lacking and the plants suffer, they will.

The addition of fertilizer to the fruit tree is a subject of debate by gardeners as well as orchardists. There are those who suggest that you let the tree be completely unaffected until there's a major limitation to its growth. On the other hand, others believe that regular fertilization is useful and essential.

Although commercial growers are regularly fertilized however, most home-grown growers discover that their trees require low amounts of fertilization. The best way to plan fertilization is according to the pattern of growth that the plant is experiencing. If the tree is growing well and its nutritional requirements are being fulfilled and fertilization is not required. If the performance of your tree is not as good or the plant appears spindly and weak, there is a possibility to apply a nitrogen-rich fertilizer during the early spring. The best option is to apply organic matter that naturally occurs to achieve this (for examples, alfalfa or composted manure from poultry) since commercial fertilizers often cause burning to the roots of young trees and cause more harm than beneficial.

After planting, fertilize your fruit trees during the spring by raking away the mulch, and then rubbing an organic fertilizer that is balanced in the soil (follow guidelines for application as indicated on the label of the product). Add a mulch made of wood for bringing the mulch's depth up to 4 inches four-foot circles around the bottom on the trees.

Pruning

The primary purpose behind pruning fruit trees is to control the growth rate, increase yields, and improve the fruit's size and the quality. The most effective way to think about pruning is that you're helping your tree concentrate the entire growing and fruiting energies to more targeted strategies. The tree that is pruned and the unpruned plant have similar sources of energy to produce fruits. However, when you trim your tree, it will be able to focus more on the fruits left, so it grows bigger, more durable and healthier.

A majority of pruning takes place during dormant seasons usually just before growing activity begins in the spring. It can extend into the blooming stage. Bees can be problematic when the plant is blooming. At this time the wounds from pruning are healed and sealed quickly. blossom buds can be more readily recognized, and injuries due to cold temperatures in winter will be averted.

The majority of pruning in the summer is used to train trees to form (spalling) and also to promote narrow, small and short development (however any pruning can have an effect of dwarfing). In order to ensure the highest yield of fruit be careful when pruning, taking out just as necessary to create an established structure that is able to support large fruit without causing harm and with enough room for sunlight and air access. This will ensure a healthy development of the fruit development and also more effective the control of pests.

Make sure you are cautious about the frequency and amount you cut your trees. Pruning excessively can cause your trees to weaken spindly, prone to insects. Pruning at the incorrect time of the year could cause those wounds that were cut during pruning to not heal properly and close and cause opening wounds to the trees, which can make the trees weak and vulnerable.

There are many various styles of pruning which work well with different varieties of trees. For apple and cherry trees, a technique known as Central-Leader trim is the most common method utilized. Central leaders are the trunk that is the central part of the tree, from which the branches that are offset to the side develop. The method is used to trim the branch laterals while leaving the central branch unharmed. Open-Center pruning can be used on plants like peaches in which there does not have a dominant vertical tree (a central leader). Open-center pruning is built around four or three main branches that are placed at wide angles and the smaller branches of five or six each.

The apple responds well to trimming. It is important to cut off the branches that are broken as well. If the tree is brimming with unnecessary branches, cut off most of the branches. It is a good idea to leave 5-8 branches around the branch. If they are more than 2 feet (24 inches) then cut them back up to 18-24 inches. The branch with the lowest length must not be more than 24 inches to the soil the line. If the tree is brimming with many high branches take them off or cut these branches. Also, you should remove branches with a narrow angle which extends in parallel with the central leader. In the ideal situation, your tree should form a pattern like a pyramid the tree trunk.

A properly maintained tree will possess a slender shape this means there should be branches that are perpendicular to the central leader, which encircles the tree. The spacing should be around 24 inches of space between the branches in order for sufficient illumination to cover every level of the tree. The branches that are the lowest are supposed to be between 24 and 36 inches away from the soil distance.

For peaches, an open center (or vase-shaped) is suggested for the best sun exposure, the highest yield, and for the highest quality peaches. Pruning of peach trees must be completed in the year prior to beginning the plant and each year after that to make sure that there is a balance between an established framework and the growth of the vegetation and production of fruit.

Similar to other kinds of trees, you'll want to begin pruning low hanging, damaged or dead branches initially. Then, take out any upward shoots that are growing along the tree's scaffolds, which are located in the interior and can possibly shade areas in the central. The second and third year take down any hanging, damaged or dead branches, as well as any upright shoots with a lot of energy which are growing within the tree (the inner part of the vase) and make sure you keep the shorter shoots around for the production of fruit.

An important tip for peach trees If you live in a mild winter, cold winters (no freezing or frost damage) there will be more peaches bloom than the tree is able to take and need to be trimmed down to avoid any injury to the tree in later the season. About 3-4 weeks after flowering (or when the biggest fruit on the tree is approximately half the size of a quarter). Then, remove the fruits by hand ensuring that all remaining fruit are placed about 8 inches apart. The thinness of this method will not only shield the tree from falling down and possible branch damage but also permits the non-culled fruit to

develop optimal dimension and the
quality.

Chapter 3: Pest and Disease Tips

There are many bugs and diseases that could possibly affect fruit trees, including diverse insects, animals like deer and birds or fungi and areas near potentially conflicts between species (like trees that are afflicted by cedars, causing the peach blight and other species that alter the pH of soil that you trees). They are most vulnerable to diseases and pests while they're new and beginning to establish (before they start to produce begin to produce fruit) however, the issues may affect your tree anytime time. Since fungi and insects can be very infectious it is important to take care to treat the problem quickly in order so that you can stop the spread of the disease on nearby trees.

It is recommended to make it a practice to check your trees regularly in search of signs of animal activity or insect activity on the leaves, on branches or the trunk as well as any signs that show signs of mildew, mold, and rot or blighting on the bark or the leaves. There are many possibilities for problems, it's important that you discover signs that something is unusual, keep a record of the findings and investigate the specific bug or disease.

However, in general, there are steps that can be taken to limit or prevent a significant amount of insect activity from your trees. It is important to protect the trunk of your trees from rodents or rabbits through girdling. This is done by using a spiral guard mostly made of white plastic. White color can also help to protect from winter-related traumas. If you opt to do this it is recommended that the guards be taken off in summer so that they do not create an safe habitat for insects that bore into trunks. Alternately, you could paint the trunk using clear latex (you may add a small amount of sand in order to repel rodents and rabbits too) and tie an 18-inch section of galvanized hardware fabric over the trunk. It isn't necessary to remove it. The deer are able to be stopped from harming the delicate shoots as well as the leaves and fruits by hanging scent-related objects in the trees (small soap bars and cloth bags with human hair, etc.). It can be temporary solution but in the event that there is still a problem with deer then sturdy tall fencing is the best solution for the damage caused by deer.

Birds are fond of fruit they can decimate the trees that produce fruit before you notice the damage. Cherry trees are a favorite of birds! The most efficient and effective method to discourage birds is to use fine mesh nets that covers the top on the trees. It is important to ensure that the netting is not too fine that birds aren't in a trap trying to access the fruit. It's a good idea but it is difficult to implement with normal size trees or semi dwarfs which have become way too large to fill. There is also the option of creating 'net cages' by constructing an ungainly wooden box or frame around the trees and connect netting on the frame.

Some other methods of deterring birds include aluminum pie tins, sound makers and even lures for predators (like snakes or owls) However, the majority of birds become accustomed to the techniques.

Harvesting

Determining Ripeness

When apples are ripe, the release of a hormone known as the ethylene. The hormone affects some cells which divide in the fruit stem and the spur of fruit (where it is derived from). The abscission layer. When the fruit is ripe it weakens this layer and the fruit will ultimately fall off the tree. The strength of the bond varies between different species, but some such as Gala are very sturdy connection, and they remain on the tree for longer when they are ripe. Others, such as Spartan or Gravenstein are much less strong in their bond, and are more likely to fall when they are not fully ripe. The fruit that is the most favorable sunlight exposure upper branches or on the south-facing part of the tree or on young trees with large branches, are likely to develop in the beginning. Choose those that are ready and return after a couple of days to look for ones that were still not ripe at the time of first pick.

The quickest method to judge the ripeness of apples is to slice a piece of in half horizontally and then examine the seeds. Most of the time, in late ripening varieties as the seeds begin to turn brown the fruit has reached its ripeness however with the

early-season apples, they could be eating
by the time the seeds start turning brown.

The test for starch is an excellent indicator
of the the ripeness of apple. The more an
apple matures its starches gradually
convert to sugars. This usually happens
beginning at the core and moving towards
the outer. Choose an apple to test then
cut it in half vertically, and spray the apple
with a light solution of iodine. If iodine is
spray, cells with starch stain dark.
However, it doesn't react with cells with
sugar. This can be a visible indicator of the
state of maturation.

The test for starch is one of the most
simple and most effective indicators to the
backyard grower. If the only area in the

core is free of starch and the remainder is dark, then the fruit is typically unripe and unripe. Any fruit that you intend to preserve should be picked in the time that one-half to three-quarters the cross section of your sample is free of starch. If the majority of the cross-section is devoid of starch then it's too mature for long-term storage and is best consumed and processed, or kept for a for a short time only. Once you've determined the ripeness of the fruit, select only those fruits similar to the ones you have examined, and using other signals such as hue (how many reds a particular red variety is and green changing to yellow)

Make sure you dispose all iodine-treated fruit.

For the majority of stone fruits, it's time to pick once the fruit has begun to color nicely and is beginning to begin to soften. In general, a tasting test can be an excellent indication at this time too. Nectarines and peaches typically tend to soften initially on the suture line which extends between the stem and the flower in the peach (the blossom can be found in the opposite direction). The area is gently pressed using your fingers to test whether it is softening. The color breaks in the ground are an additional method of confirming whether the fruit is ripe. Select the fruit when the color breaks occur - the moment a fruit changes between greenish and yellow,(or for cream-colored white flesh peaches). If you harvest the fruit in the wrong time, you are at the chance of getting lower-quality fruits that do not mature completely. It is common to find an unappetizing and sour peaches in the supermarket you've probably picked it in the wrong time. Certain varieties are somewhat firm, even after they are mature, so make sure to look into the specific cultivar you've chosen to get more specific tips.

When it comes to pears, they can be classified in two categories of European varieties: the fall pears that don't require storage time prior to usage, and winter pear which will not develop effectively if they're not provided with a time of rest during cold storage following the harvest. Some of the most sought-after early-ripening varieties for autumn pears are Bartlett and Orcas and later-ripening winter pear varieties are Bosc as well as Highland.

Whatever the case, the winter and fall pears remain "green" once they're in the process of harvesting. If you hold off too long to appear ripe (with yellow-colored skin) they'll be extremely fragile and may quickly turn to rotting during storage. Additionally, because many pears mature in the middle (like apples) the pears that have been ripened by the tree will turn brown in the middle and become overripe. Naturally, this will be specific to the variety, however this is a common occurrence with all apples in the fall. Orcas is one of them. Orcas is a particular species that hasn't been vulnerable to this problem, however it is ripe when it is on the tree. (However the ripening process isn't recommended in any kind of variety if you intend to keep it for longer than a brief time prior to use or storage).

One of the best ways to determine whether a pear is mature enough to harvest is that the stems should easily break away from the spur once the pear is removed (just similar to apples). If you struggle with a twang or pull in order to take the pear off the tree, then it's generally not ripe enough. Following harvest, pears from fall are able to be stored on a shelf in a temperatures at room temperature until the fruit matures fully (when the yellow hue develops and the fruit starts to become soft). They can also be preserved however, do not store them longer than 4-6 weeks. They are perfect for drying, canning or any other method of preservation. They should be placed straight from the pick to cold storage (temperature can vary between 40F and 33F) and then stored there for at least 3 weeks. After that, it is time getting them at room temperature so that they can finish the process of softening. For the initial batch of winter pears, it could require a few days to completely ripen. However, in the future, a couple of days in room temperature will suffice.

(A excellent suggestion is to record of when you pick your trees year after year. In general, they be harvested in the first week of season of harvest every year. So, you could begin testing the fruits one couple of weeks prior to the expected harvest date in the end, you'll have a good understanding of your trees to be able to harvest them without any difficulty.)

Cold Storage

In the long-term storage of fruit one of the main things to do is keep the fruits dry, cool (but not overly dry!) and aerated. This slows the process of fruit respiration. This slows the process of cell breakdown and rotting. Ventilation prevents ethylene gas and carbon dioxide from accumulating at levels that speed up the process of spoilage. (Important noting: Ethylene encourages ripening in nearby fruits. If you'd like to make sure that a couple of pieces which are more ripe to eat Place an apple into an airtight bag and add some other fruit like apples and keep an eye on it frequently). If properly stored, a lot of fruit can last for a long time using this technique!

It is crucial to control moisture since moist environments can cause decay. A variety of options to address this issue are a shed or garage as well as a heated porch dry basements, or the dry cellar. Beware of direct sunlight and areas where temperatures fluctuate. Avoid areas with no ventilation (like plastic storage containers or bags made of plastic). Fruits may be stored in containers with adequate air circulation, and filled with paper or padding. Beware of stacking peaches or other fruits with soft flesh in more than 2 layers. In doing so, you could bruise and harm the fruits which can lead to a faster loss of the fruit. Beware of storing fruits that have visible blemishes since they could serve as a source for rotting. Be sure to check your fruits regularly for any rotten or spoilt fruit and take them out immediately. If you've ever been told that "One bad apple can ruin the entire bunch" that's what the saying was about. The rot quickly spreads among tightly kept fruits. But if properly harvested and preserved, apples as well as the pears are able to be enjoyed long after the harvest season has ended.

Canning

The process of canning is just as exciting and satisfying as preparing the fruit! A little planning, and a time to prepare is all it takes for a great food item all through the year. There are a variety of methods to prepare fruit to can, and the recipes are readily accessible. A few options include jellies preserves, jams and preserves, either half- or even whole (in either heavy or light syrup). Also, you will require a canning jar (Mason or Ball brands are the best) lids, lids, screw tops and the water bath or pressure canner (for the more sophisticated homemade canners!) The jars must be cleaned with soapy water and cleaned thoroughly and then kept warm. It is crucial since it stops the growth of bacteria in the jars and also prevents the breaking during the process of canning.

Raw Pack (Cold Pack)

Put uncooked (washed and cut) fruits in jars and overflow with hot boiling fruit juice, sugar syrup, or water. There should be an opening between the lids and food items or drinks. The head space is essential for bubbling liquids as well as the expansion of fruit. If the jars are overflowing, they could spill out during the process. The head space is typically somewhere between 1/8 to 1/2 inches. Make sure to check the specific recipe you're using for how much head space.

Hot Pack

Make syrup by heating the fruit under steam or in water prior to packaging. Fruits with higher juice content may be heated prior to packing without liquid before being packed into the juice, which is cooked out.

Each jar should be packed with a minimum of 1/4 inch its top or in accordance with the each recipe. If the food is not liquid (ie. fruit like peaches) it is important to eliminate any air bubbles using an elongated rubber spatula or table knife lightly between the solid food as well as the edge of the Jar. Pour in more syrup if necessary. Clean screw threads and rim with a damp, clean cloth. Place lid over top, and screw bands onto it securely and evenly to keep the sealer lid made of rubber (or sealing rings) to the jar. It is sometimes essential to place and secure the lid down while you make sure that you tighten the band so that the lid sits at the surface of the container. Be careful not to over-tighten. Jars can then be put in the rack inside the hot water canner.

Rack the jars immediately after packing. Then, lower the filled rack into the canner. Jars need to be covered by about 2 to 1 inch of water. You can add boiling water as you require. If you want to add additional water, make sure to divide the pots but not directly onto the jars (this is where the additional hot water kettle is useful). The lid must be secured to the pot. As soon as the water reaches an unending boil, begin to record the cooking time. Cook slowly and gently to the time that is recommended for the product that is being cooked. After the boiling time has expired, take the containers at once, and then place on a rack or towels that are away from hot air and from airflow.

Once the jars have been cooled for between 12 to 24 hours following the process, make sure you check the seal. In order to do this, press downwards on the middle on the lid. The lid should con-cave and will not move once you press. Another option is to tap the lid using the bottom of one teaspoon. If the jar has been sealed properly, it will create a loud, high pitched sound. If it produces a sluggish sound, it indicates that the lid has not been closed or that the food item is touching the inside of the lid. Be cautious If within an hour or two after cooling, you can hear an explosion sound coming out of the lids. It is an excellent sound to be aware of since it is usually a sign the vacuum effect has been created which has caused the lids to break and form a seal.

Once the jars are completely cooled and cooled, screw bands can be removed, if needed. It is important to label canning jars with the contents and processing dates. Keep jars stored in a cool, dry, dark place.

Canning Tips:

Canned fruit can often slide off if the sugar syrup becomes too heavy or when jars are packed loosely, or if there is air within the tissue of the fruit following being processed. For this reason, you should make sure you use a medium or light sugar syrup. Also, ensure that the your fruit is firm, ripe and not overly ripe and then pack the fruit securely in the jars, and avoid crushing.

If the fruit isn't coated with liquid, it could become dark during storage, however this doesn't necessarily mean that it has been rotten. For this reason, make sure that you cover the fruit with liquid, but not leaving enough headspace. Make sure you remove trapped air bubbles using an elongated rubber scraper spatula, or kitchen knife. For this to be done effectively move the jar up and down as you run the knife across the top of the fruit to the edges of the jar. You can also try press the fruit inwards a couple of times.

A spoon-shaped spatula that is flat rather than rounded can be useful to mix sugar syrup in the flat bottomed pot while cooking.

Do not store canned foods near an appliance, a water heater and hot pipes for water. Jars must be stored at a cool temperature to prolong time and also to guard from spoilage. It is important to keep them in a dry area. A scuffing of the lid band could cause the seal to crack.

To prevent freezing in cold storage spaces, wrap the canning jars of canned food with newspaper, then set them inside heavy cardboard boxes. Wrap boxes in a sturdy blanket or cloth, if required.

In order to make a straightforward small amount of jam made from cherries the following ingredients are required:

3 cups chopped and pitted fresh cherries

1 cup of unsweetened apple juice

2 teaspoons of lemon juice

2 packs of powdered fruits pectin (2 2 ounces)

3 cups of white sugar

Chapter 5: Half pint canning jars that have rings and lids

Directions:

Put the cherries, apple juice as well as lemon juice and pectin in a big saucepan on a medium heat. Bring to a boil and then add the sugar. Make the jam and cook it to a simmer for about 2 minutes while continuously stirring. Removing the jam from the stove and skimming away any foam.

The lids and jars should be sterilized by boiling the lids and jars for at least five minutes. The cherry jam should be placed in the sterilized, hot Jars and then fill them up to 1/4 inch from the top. Make sure to run a knife or small spatula along the interiors of the jars once the jam has been added to eliminate the air-bubbles. The rims should be cleaned of Jars using a moist towel to get rid of the food particles. Add lids to the jars, then put on rings.

Put a rack into the middle of a huge stockpot, and then fill it halfway with water. Heat to a simmer over the highest heat. Then, slowly lower the jars in the stockpot using a pot holders. Make sure to leave a 2-inch space between the Jars. Fill the jars with additional boiling water, if needed until the level of water is at least 1 " over the tops of the containers. Bring the water to a complete boiling point, then place the pot over the top, and continue to cook for fifteen minutes.

The jars should be removed from the stockpot and put them on wooden or cloth covered surfaces separated by a few inches until they are cool. When cool, you can press the lid's top using a finger to ensure that the seal is secure (lid is not moving up or down). Keep in a cool, dark place.

(This recipe could be modified to be scaled-up for large quantities of jam.)

Drying/Dehydrating

Dehydrating fruits is a great option to preserve your produce to last for a long time. A few people achieve this feat with expensive dehydrating equipment for food however, the same effect is achievable by using your kitchen oven, wooden spoon, and cookies sheets.

In order to dehydrate the apples, you can cut the slices into chips or pieces. If you prefer make them steam, do so at first for a couple of minutes to keep the end item from becoming too hard to chew (although certain people prefer the texture a bit chewy, but less crisp). If you decide to cook them in the steamer, be sure you rinse them in cold water afterward to end the cooking process. Then, blot with paper towels in order to eliminate the excess water. Then, let them soak in an acid solution like apple juice or lemon juice. In this way, you can prevent the flesh of apples from turning an unpleasant brown hue. An ideal proportion is around 1:4 acid/water ratio. Soak the soaked vegetables for five minutes and wipe dry. When they're soaking in the oven, heat it to the lowest temperature (typically with ovens that are used for cooking at home, that is between 150 and 160°F). Put the apple chips or slices together on a baking tray (using parchment paper or aluminum foil for the barrier). Use a wooden spoon to place between the oven and its door, allowing it to open by a tiny crack. This is how the apples dry out and do not cook. Allow them to sit for several hours. Once you're unable to remove any water by pinning the fruits and they don't break when pinched (or split and fracture if you prefer their crunchy) you're done. Cool them, then store in a container that is sealed at room temperature, dry and dark location. (Tip To determine if the fruit has been totally dehydrated, grab small pieces and place them into a sandwich bag, then seal it. If there's any evidence of water or condensation the fruit isn't completely drying.)

The technique is adaptable to other fruit varieties (pears as well as halved and pitted cherries, apricots, and various kinds of plums) however, typically fruit that are less juicy can be used in this method. Peaches are far too juicy to be dehydrated effectively. They're better processed to make the form of leather made from fruit!

An easy, quick and simple recipe for fruit leather

Pick your favorite fruit (I like peaches)

Baking sheet

Aluminum foil

Wooden spoon

Blender

Pre-heat your oven to its lowest setting (typically the temperature range is between 150 and 160°F)

Cut the fruit of your you'd like into pieces of smaller size.

Mix until you have a uniform consistency. If you're mixing a fruit which is not as juicy, include a tiny amount of water to make sure it's spread uniformly.

Place the baking sheet on top of aluminum foil. Ensure it is completely covered on all sides.

Slowly pour the fruit purée onto the baking sheet, periodically moving the tray around to ensure that the mix disperses evenly.

Place in oven preheated.

Close the oven door and leave an open space using the spoon made of wood (this is essential so the fruit can dehydrate, and but not cooks).

Make sure to check every now and then until water has evaporated completely. The time range is between 3 and 12 hours according to the precise temperatures of the oven and the amount of water present in the fruit (juicier fruits require longer time to dry than dry ones.) I've observed that the average is 5-6 hours.

Chapter 6: Which Kind of Fruit Tree Should You Plant?

Take into consideration these two aspects in deciding on the kind of tree to cultivate:

1) The weather

2) Your tastes

There is a way to combat the cold by growing your plants in a conservatory, or even a heated greenhouse. However, it will be expensive. The majority of people prefer to plant any fruit tree that will thrive in their particular climate.

There is a good chance that you already be aware of the fruit trees can thrive in your area by watching what neighbors or farmers from the area you live in are cultivating. There is an organic farm and see which fruit trees are growing on display or look for a local nursery or a family-run garden center, that allows you to talk with them about the varieties that will thrive depending on where you live.

Another thing to think about is pollination for the trees. If you don't have any other fruit trees within the area you might be able to benefit by purchasing several varieties of the same fruit trees, instead of any of a variety in order that your plants are able to pollinate one another. In the event that they do not, your trees could be unable to bear fruit due to insects aren't able to pollinate them.

It is also important to think about the height to which your trees are likely to get, and this is a subject we'll talk about later. Even though you'll delight at the harvesting of the fruits you grow yourself however, they could get high enough that they block the view of your home and neighbors property. Don't start an argument because your trees block your house from light!

Every type of fruit will usually have several types. As an example there are hundreds varieties of apple varieties that range in size from Pink Lady up to Pippen up to Granny Smith, Golden Delicious, Braeburn and more. With such a wide array of possibilities, it's entirely your choice to pick the one you'd prefer to cultivate.

There are many who believe that indigenous varieties of fruits that are not produced commercially can be a wise choice since they are more flavorful and differ from other varieties. You can certainly grow common varieties of apples. However, they are also available at your local supermarket. However, if you're growing a traditional breed, you'll be able to have access to one that's difficult to locate. Therefore, if you're looking to be curious, try growing an unusual variety of the fruit family.

There are usually fruits trees on the internet or in nearby garden stores. The trees can be bought in bare roots or as containers. Though bare root plants are likely to be less expensive however, they also have a higher mortality rate due to the fact that they have been without soil for an extended time that can cause harm to the plants. As they are inspected by the plants before purchasing they and take care of them and properly, they will have the ability to thrive.

Be sure the plant you select to plant in your garden will be a good fit for your area and can make it through the winter months. There are times when you can help the plants to withstand winter by covering them with an insulated fleece. However, this does not necessarily work for fruit trees, especially in winter when it is extremely cold.

Choose the fruits you're interested in as well as ones that you and your family members enjoy eating. This way that when you begin to harvest the fruits, not a single one will go into waste, and it can be enjoyed by all!

What To Look For When Choosing Fruit Trees

The fruit trees do not come with a wide variety of species and shapes, they also come in a broad assortment of shapes and sizes. There are the patio plant, large trees and saplings, medium-sized trees and more. Which one to decide on and which one is right for your yard and backyard?

If you're deciding between plant varieties that are bare roots, or grow in pots Be aware that plants growing inside containers typically are of superior in quality, even however they may be higher priced. If you're purchasing big trees, they'll usually be bare-root trees because they're specially cultivated for your needs. At garden shops, you're most likely to come across fruits trees in container soil.

Although you are able to cultivate fruit trees by seed however, the majority of store-bought fruits will be propagated by the rootstock. This is quite common. A particular kind of fruit tree is transplanted on the roots of another plant, usually one of the kind.

It's often used to create a tree that is more resistant to disease, or even for the growth of smaller trees. As an example, you'll typically see pear trees grafted on quince rootstocks because quinces are larger than pear plants. This makes it possible to grow a smaller pear tree.

The kind of rootstock used determines how large the tree gets as well as how deep-rooted the plant is, the degree of resistance it is against pests or diseases, as well as the climate, and how long it takes to produce fruit, and so on.

Three types of rootstocks are normal (which yields a fully-grown tree) as well as semi-dwarf (trees with a height of 2-4 meters high) as well as dwarf (where the trees are no taller that 2.5 metres).

Most of the time the fruit trees you have require to be crossed pollinated by another species of tree. Certain varieties of fruit trees can be self-fertile. However there is a great benefit by the presence of a different trees.

Different kinds of trees bloom at different times throughout the year. It is possible that buying two distinct kinds of apple trees they will not be blooming in the exact time in the same season. Be sure the apple trees that you purchase bloom in the same time so that you get the most pollination, and the most productive yield.

The majority of fruit trees thrive in sunny locations However, many prefer to be protected so that they're protected from the high temperatures and the late frost.

Be aware that different kinds of fruits have different tastes. Are you a fan of cooking apples, or dessert apples? Apples that are sweet or tangier apples? There are a variety that you could consider how you would like to utilize the fruit you grow and how this can affect the trees you choose to plant.

Check how tall the tree will rise to as you'll want easily harvest your fruits and trim the trees.

In the final day, if confused about which option to pick You can always seek advice by contacting one of the numerous gardening websites or ask for help at your neighborhood garden store owned by family members.

Growing Fruit Trees in Containers

It is possible that you don't have the area to grow an orchard, or perhaps a large tree. There may be no room for a yard, but a tiny space, or perhaps a balcony and what else can you accomplish to cultivate fruits in your in your own home?

Do not worry about it; regardless of what space you're given there is still a way to plant trees. Did you remember in the last chapter we discussed dwarf trees that can only reach around 2.5 meters in height? It is possible to get much smaller trees today as small or small patio trees.

This type of tree is ideal for those with a smaller space in which to plant the plants as they be able to thrive in containers and will not grow more than an meter in the most. The type of tree isn't inclined to expand outwards. i.e. it is vertically growing with no spreading branches. If it starts to spread branches, all you have do is prune it to prevent the growth from spreading more.

Mini trees produce a tiny quantity of fruits, but the fruits are still delicious. They usually grow near to the trunk.

There are dwarf and even regular trees in pots but if they become to large for their pots, they may suffer, and yield of fruit can decrease. This is one of the reasons to select a small or patio tree if the area is very restricted.

If you plant fruits in containers, they require more care than those which are planted in the ground as their roots are contained, and they are not able to access water and food sources.

The planting of your fruit trees with the soil mix of vermiculite and compost (or perlite) can give an increased chance of being successful in the containers they are placed in. The tree will benefit from an abundance of water that is retained by the soil and nutritious food sources from the compost. So if you choose to use the slow release fertilizer it can save you from needing to feed your tree over a period of time.

Also, you should think about the materials you will use for the container. Clay containers provide greater stability because of their mass, but are more prone to drying out as compared to a plastic container and are better in retaining the moisture. The end of the day, it is dependent on the location you would like the pots to go and the style you want it to have.

Repotting your plants each several years, generally at the end of fall or in earlier in winter when the leaves have fallen can keep them from becoming pot bound. When they've reached their the full extent of their size and have reached their final pot, you can trim the roots each two years. You can replace approximately a third of your compost each year to help it will flourish.

Another benefit of cultivating fruit trees in container gardens is the ability to move your plants about. If you're cultivating delicate plants, such as apricots They aren't fond of cold weather and are able to be moved in the conservatory or greenhouse during the winter months.

Planting fruit trees in container gardens is an excellent method of obtaining fresh fruit within your home if you are faced with little space. It's a simple method to maintain the trees, and it requires minimal maintenance when you establish your trees in a proper manner.

Chapter 7: Planting Your Fruit Trees

If you're able to simply dig an opening and plant your tree in the ground, it is better to ensure that your tree gets the best chance to flourish by planting them correctly. Trees with bare roots in particular must be planted properly in order to develop a strong root system that will produce high harvests of fruit.

The main issues with new fruit trees are those that occur beneath the ground. It is essential to ensure that the tree receives adequate nutrients and enough water in the initial few months following the planting. It is your primary goal for your tree established with an established root system, to ensure it will grow healthy, strong branches and fruits.

Timing is the most important aspect of this procedure and it's ideal to plant your fruits trees towards the close of winter, or in the initial days of spring. The ground has not frozen and is easier to get the tree planted. Also, trees that are dormant in the winter months, begin to develop to a point where your tree is at the ideal location to make the most of the site it is now in.

It is possible to determine the ideal time to begin planting new trees based on the manner in which they appear at garden shops within your region. If you're ordering naked roots, it is important to put them in the ground quickly once they arrive.

If you don't meet this period, container-based trees could be planted later on at the end of the year. Since these trees are established in the soil, they can normally be resistant to being planted again in the event that you do not cause damage to the roots during the planting process.

The one thing that fruit trees dislike is having to be moved after they have been planted. Therefore, it's essential to choose the best location. Keep in mind that the majority of fruit trees prefer full sunlight However, there are a few kinds that are tolerant of some shade.

A majority of fruit trees do not prosper in locations that dry out the soil excessively or where there is a are flooded. The best soil to grow them is one that drains freely and is fertilized with high quality compost. If the soil in your garden isn't adequate, then consider enhancing and conditioning it to make sure it's.

Also, be aware that fruit trees aren't a fan of extreme winds, or huge amounts of snow falling on the trees, i.e. due to snow falling off of an roof. It can harm the fruit tree, and strong winds can cause fruit to drop before they're completely ripe. There is a possibility of stakes your tree, especially when it's smaller, so it develops a solid root system, without winds inflicting too much stress on it.

If there are other plant species in the vicinity of your fruit trees, be aware that they could battle for water and food so you must ensure that you ensure that your plants are watered and fertilized frequently to make sure they will grow vigorously.

For the first time, it is important to give to your tree's fruit more attention that you do after it has established. Make sure you water the plant during hot and dry weather. If the temperature is extremely hot, make sure your tree gets the chance to soak thoroughly rather than only a superficial watering. Make sure to keep the roots of the tree clear of grass and roots, so it has little competition the tree. The mulch mat can be helpful in this situation.

At the beginning of your first year, it's very important that it is removed from the tree, too. There is a possibility that you would like to see some fruits grow in the trees as quickly as you can. However, by removing the bloom it will reduce strain on your tree. The tree will concentrate its efforts to develop a healthy root system that will provide the tree with a stronger, healthier tree which can produce more productive crops in the future.

The simplest way to plant your fruit tree:

1)Create a hole sufficient for the tree's roots to grow without breaking them. It should be deep enough so that the roots and the beginning inch of your trunk are covered by soil.

2)The soil should be loose at the edge of the hole to ensure that roots expand more easily.

3)Put the tree in the middle of the bore. Check for the graft joint in which the rootstock is fitted to the trunk and make sure that it's at the ground.

4)Make sure to fill in the hole using the dirt you dug. There is the option of adding compost, if you like however not in excess. The soil should be gently pushed downwards to make sure that your hole is completely filled with soil and that the soil is and well-compressed. Fill the hole by layering it and then watering every layer to remove air pockets as well as to help the soil become more compact.

5)In addition to the remaining soil, you can create an elevated circle of soil approximately four feet across the entire bottom of your tree. This will help keep the water in the bottom of the tree while you water it.

If you're planting rootless trees, this should be completed sooner then later. Bare root trees benefit from being submerged in water for several hours prior to being planted.

Feeding and Watering Your Fruit Trees

If you have just planted a fruit tree, it is require watering them regularly in the season of growth. It is crucial for a tree that was just planted and also for the initial couple of years in its existence.

In hot weather, it is necessary to water your plants more frequently. If you're making use of a drip irrigation system then you might need to add several drippers in order to completely cover the root zone.

In winter months, you don't have to water your trees often, if none at all. If it is rainy for some time then you'll need to provide water however, otherwise, they'll do fine.

Once your trees are established, it will be less necessary to water them as frequently, maybe only once every 2 or 3 weeks. If there is severe heat waves that is expected, you'll need to water them frequently and even after they have been established.

In the last week of February or the first week in March, once your fruit trees start coming out of winter dormancy, they will require fertilization your trees. When the fruit has begun to been ripe, it's important to fertilize them again, at the end of summer, to stimulate them to create new branches for coming year. If you wish to boost the growth of fruitwood during this time it is possible to make use of a fertilizer rich in nitrogen.

The winter months (from to the close of October to the beginning of November) it is also possible to fertilize your fruit trees at least once each month through the month of January. It allows for fertilizers to be built up for the tree to utilize in the beginning of growth in the spring.

You should be generous when it comes to fertilizing in particular when the tree is mature. It will guarantee that your trees will thrive and bear the fruits you desire.

The mature trees may be free to roam however, to increase the amount of fruit you produce and ensure that your trees are healthy, you should spend some time irrigation and fertilization. But, they do not require the same amount of attention as the other kinds of trees and tend to be more solitary than other vegetables.

Keep watch on them and take care of them and they'll provide an abundance of tasty fruit.

Chapter 8: How to Successfully Prune Fruit Trees

A crucial aspect of keeping an enviable fruit tree is trimming. It is the process of cutting off branches that are not needed and then shape the tree. If you are a novice to the art of keeping fruit trees it can be an intimidating process.

In the initial five years you own your fruit trees, be sure to prune it to the form you would like, to ensure that it develops in the manner you'd like to see it. It is important to ensure that there aren't more than it needs in this time to let it concentrate its efforts to its own development, and ensure that it will bear of healthy fruit to come in the near future.

Open Bush Trees

This is the most common form of home-grown pruning which results in a tree with a shape like a goblet with an open area at the top. When you purchase the tree, it has been already cut to a certain degree and you are able to select one that has been goblet-shaped, giving you the advantage.

Fruit trees can be feathered (with sides shoots) or are unfeathered (without sides shoots).

If you are pruning during winter Cut the branches just before the buds. It's best to check that you have strong buds across the branch. Make sure to take time to take the time to form the tree to the form of a goblet, and eliminate branches growing outwards.

Every winter, you are able to trim your tree in order to give it a more pleasing shape making sure that it's free of any growing on the interior. If the tree you have is becoming excessively sagging, you could trim some branches in order to make it grow out of the buds to what you desire. If your branches have grown into the center of the tree, you could completely take them off through cutting them to a flush with the branch that they grow from.

Apples and pears are more prone to be cut back in winter. However, plants like Apricots, plums, and cherries are best pruned during the summertime. If you have large, then pruning will require more effort in particular if it was inherited the tree when you first moved into your new home. It is possible to purchase a specific "paint" to apply over the branches after pruning them in order to guard the tree against disease.

Pruning more mature trees can be the fact that a tree might become infected due to the wound as that's exactly what happens for the tree as far as it is involved. If you can seal the wound, it will protect the tree. For younger trees, this may not be so important, however you can do it when you wish to ensure that your tree is healthy.

Cordon PruningThis is an type of pruning that is more common in smaller gardens, where you cultivate your trees using walls or a trellis. The branches of the tree climb up the wall and bear fruit.

When you are ready to plant the fruit trees, you need to attach the wire with a strong connection across the wall. They should be at least 1 foot (30cm) away and should be at a height of 2 feet (60cm) over the soil.

The best way to do this is to plant the tree approximately 6 inches (15cm) away from the wall, and then anchor it with a cane which is tied to wires (or put it behind the wires in case you plan to get rid of it later on).

When you've set the wires in your tree, trim the branches on either side to four branches at a level distance from the wires. It is not advisable to take the top off on the tree before it's reached the height that you wish it to reach.

After the initial summer following planting, cut off the entire bloom so that the plant is focused on growth rather than producing fruits. Then, in the winter, trim the branches on either side up to three buds, to promote the growth of more buds.

Espaliers

Another type of pruning which is perfect for fences or walls. It is also recommended to plant the tree about the distance of six inches (15cm) to the wall. You then fix the tree to a horizontal structure usually wires, but it could be railings and fence posts.

In the spring Choose the primary branch, and then train two of its shoots to develop along the horizontal support. If more shoots develop then cut down to three leaves in June, or completely remove them.

After the winter break choose two more branches you want to build on a horizontal support that is about 18 inches (45cm) higher than the wire below. Reduce the main tree to an ear about two inches (5cm) over this level.

Continue this procedure the next year and do this until you reach the size you desire with the fruit tree.

This kind of tree on the grounds of English estates, which is stunning. This is an excellent option to make boring fence or wall exciting and also productive!

By using these methods of pruning, you will be capable of growing healthy trees for fruit that will provide plenty of delicious fruits for you. When you prune your tree, you will keep it healthy while making it much easier to harvest the fruits.

Propagating Your Fruit Trees

The first thing you'll like to accomplish is producing additional fruit trees. It is possible to grow them by seeding them, however this is a long and arduous process as anyone who's attempted it can be able to attest. If you're determined to stay for the long-term and willful to care for your plant with patience, it's definitely feasible to create the fruit trees you want from seeds. It could also make for a great project.

But, the most well-known method of growing fruits is to plant the cuttings from. When you trim your tree, instead of placing your branches in compost, they could be planted and grow to create new trees.

The tree will require an herbicide to help root your tree however, these can be accessible online or at the local garden shop. The method works for almost every kind of fruit tree However, be sure to get permission from the owner when you're using cuttings of the tree that you don't have!

If you are planting smaller trees, it is recommended to use cuttings between 4 and 8 inches, and in larger trees you should want the cuttings to be between 10 and 15 inches in length. Less mature trees usually grow quicker. If you're taking pieces, you should cut them in a 45-degree angle in order to assist the roots to take root.

Place a container of soil in it and let it get a bit moist by spraying it with a gun. The pot must be large enough that you can make the hole of eight inches deep in the bottom. If you use a 14-inch diameter pot, there are four pieces of cutting.

Cut off the bark gently off the lower third of the cutting. Put this portion of the cut into the water in a glass, being sure that the bark-free section of the cut is submerged. Put it into the water for about 5 minutes.

Then, you dip the portion of the cutting that is free of bark in the powder that acts as a rooting hormone and put it in the hole you made in the past. It is important to spread your cuttings equally if you plant multiple in one pot.

The soil should be gently pressed down over the cut pieces and then spray them with a generous mist using your water sprayer. Place the pot in the bag in white and secure the lid. Make sure to mist the interior of the bag before you tie the top.

Place the pot in a place that is out of direct light because it can dry out the soil and ruin the cutting. Choose a location that will still receive some light, but not being in the shadows of lighting and dark.

Every two days, it is necessary to mist the cut flowers again. But if your soil appears dry (it may crack when dry) Mist it regularly throughout the throughout the day. Avoid overwatering your cut flowers since they'll rot and don't take the plant from its pot in order to see how the root is progressing.

Within a few months it will be apparent that the trees are growing leaves as well as new shoots that means they've been established themselves successfully. The process may be longer in larger trees. So, take your time and be patient.

If the trees are big enough to warrant planting outside You can place them exactly where you'd like for them to expand. Do not plant them when you begin to see signs of growth. Wait at least three or four months prior to placing them in the garden.

Take care of the plants like you would any other newly-grown tree. After a couple of years, and you'll enjoy delicious fruit that you have grown yourself of your newly planted trees!

The propagation of your fruit trees as it is an excellent option to increase the number of trees are in your yard or to plant an individual type of tree at no cost that you may have been able to admire in the home of a neighbour, friend or a family member.

Chapter 9: Harvesting Your Fruit

As summer ends and the days begin to turn into autumn, the actual job begins to harvest the fruit. Then immediately the tree is brimming with the fruit which is ready and ready to be picked.

A majority of fruits will mature in the trees, but certain fruit, like peaches will be most effective if they are picked prior to when they're ripe, and then allowed to mature in the kitchen. It will make them better tasting and more sweet when you go the way.

The fruit is mature when it's slightly easy to squeeze. It is also possible to determine when the fruit is done by the fact that birds be more attracted to the trees. Keep in mind that with soft fruits and cherries, you must cover your trees with nets, or else the birds will devour everything before you reach it.

In order to give you an idea of the types and times you could get your hands on, here's an overview of the fruit trees you can take advantage of and when to harvest it:

Juillet - Cherries

August - plums, cherries and early season apples

September The plums, apples of mid-season Elderberries, plums

October: pears, elderberries and mid-season apples. Also and plums

The apples of November are late in season.

These are just guidelines. It will all depend on the weather conditions and growth season to determine the time when fruit will be ripe enough to harvest. Unfortunate weather conditions can stop the fruit from ripening in the time it should be in the event that the weather was perfect.

Don't pick all the fruits on your tree at the same time. You must decide which ones you'll take and use later. But, towards the end of the season, or when there are forecasted high winds it is best to choose your fruit, and then keep it in a safe place so that it isn't damaged when it falls off the tree. Some types of fruits, like apples that drop can be utilized in the kitchen instead of going to waste.

This could require a decent amount of effort for you, especially when you're blanching, making stews or other preparations for your fruits. However, it's worthwhile as you'll have plenty to last for the rest of the year.

The firmness of cherries is heightened and the color darkens to deep red after they're ripe and available to harvest. If they're tender and soft, they're usually too ripe. If you don't net the cherries you have picked, birds will consume them and will take the cherries off of the tree in just a few hours right before they start to mature. The cherries can be taken off the tree using a single move and they should fall away effortlessly.

Apples begin falling out of the trees when they're ready to pick, and could cause damage, especially when they fall off the branch or fall upon a rough surface. Apples are ripe once they're firm. generally, the tree will be several that it is possible to select one to check in case you're not certain when it's ripe or not. Most apple trees mature at the same time and will stay in the trees for a couple of weeks, unless there is strong winds. This gives the user time to choose their fruit.

Pears should be picked while they're not ripe and then stored in a cool, well-ventilated place for a few weeks or so until they become soft and at the point of eating. The problem is that pears that have been left to mature in the trees end with a taste that is not as great.

The most important thing you can be doing is to keep an the eye at your fruit tree as the harvest is coming up so you can determine when it's time to harvest. The sun's rays or rain may really move the fruit forward, and high winds can destroy your crop If you keep an eye at your trees as well as the weather will allow you to identify the ideal time to pick your fruit.

Storing Your Fruit

One fruit tree can usually produce of fruit that you cannot even imagine eating or make use of, and you'll need to be aware of how you can store the fruits. If you're the biggest fan of apples, it is likely that you'll have a difficult time eating a fruit tree before they fall away! Keep in mind that at certain times you might be overwhelmed with apples when conditions are especially favorable. This means greater effort on your part!

The storage capacity of apples and pears is very well, in comparison to the majority of other fruit and should be kept in the refrigerator either frozen, dried, or included in the recipe. It will surprise you how many recipes made from fruits and the length of time it can remain fresh!

If you're keeping fruit that is fresh and ready to be eaten later in the season, it is best keep it in a dark, cool area. It should be kept at a temperature between 37 and 44F (or 3 to 7C as well as adequate air circulation. It is possible to fill small boxes with safe sandy material (play sand is a good choice) and put your apples inside the sand in a way they don't touch one another. Avoid storing fruit with imperfections or blemishes because they can rot, and could cause the rest of the stored fruit decay as well.

There are containers available specially designed for storage of your fruits for storage, such as wooden boxes with slats and orchard containers. They can be useful however if you own lots of trees, they isn't cheap!

In the case of storing fruits, you may wrap them with newspaper or tissue to make it easier for it to store. If you use bags made of plastic to wrap your fruits in however, you are at risk of condensation building up inside the bag. This can cause your fruit to begin to decay. You can simply pierce the bag to prevent this from occurring.

A majority of people keep some of their fruits fresh, and use the remainder to create products, that they'll use over the year.

Make sure to check your fruit frequently after you've stocked it up since if it begins to turn brown, it may be a threat to your entire collection in no time. Check that the fruits are still in good condition and hasn't shrunk. If it's shriveled this, then it indicates that it is either too hot or that it's too dry. If that is the case, wet your floor just every week to ensure that there's an air of moisture.

When it comes to apples, early-season apple varieties aren't very suitable to keep. In mid-season, apples are usually stored for roughly five weeks. However, later season apples may be kept for several months, and their taste often gets better with time.

Take your apples to the market and take them care when handling them so they aren't damaged or smashed by any means, since it can cause them to decay. Wrap your apples with newspapers or tissue paper to keep them more fresh. It is important to ensure that your apples don't touch one the other while you're keeping them in the fridge as this could make them more susceptible to rotting.

Pears are the most fragile fruit, and they prefer to not wraps. They are typically stored for a couple of weeks therefore you'll need to be quick in taking them in. Keep the pears in an air-tight and well-ventilated area and then transfer them to a warmer location approximately a week prior to when the time to consume in order to continue to ripen.

It is an ideal method to store fresh fruits for weeks, or sometimes, even many months later, once the season of growing has ended. Although apples and peaches store quite well, different fruit will require processing in a certain method before they can be kept.

Drying Fruits

Drying fruits is an excellent option to store your fruit and is a great option if you have excess of one particular kind of fruit. It is a great snack as a snack on their own, or they can be included in a range of dishes. There are instances where their flavor may improve if the fruits are dried (sun dried tomatoes, as an instance) or even entirely, like the instance when it comes to raisins.

Drying your fruits can be done using an oven or buy the dehydrator. If you want to sundry your the fruit, it's an enormous task for the backyard grower.

Drying in the oven works best when combined with apples and tomatoes, and other fruit. Choose a low temperature oven that is 130C, 250F, or gas Mark 1. Slice your fruit cleanly, wash it and cut the pieces very thin and place the fruits in only one single layer on a baking tray. Put it into the oven until dry. It could take several hours. The fruit can be stored in an airtight container but remember to utilize it within several weeks.

Dehydrators can be an enormous time savings and can be found in many different sizes, dependent on how you would like to dry all at once. It is important to place the dehydrator in a place with a adequate airflow to ensure that moisture is absorbed from it and is not reused.

The fruit should be placed in single layers on the tray following the guidelines given by the company. The fruits are dried properly.

Be sure to wash the fruit thoroughly and eliminate the bruises, pips or stems prior to dehydrating the fruit. It is recommended to dry the fruits with cloths before putting it into the dryer. There is no need to cut the fruit like the pears, apples as well as citrus fruits or all fruits that have a stone prior to drying it. Also, make sure you chop the fruits into pieces similar in size, to ensure it's dried equally.

The fruit can be dipped in juice of pineapple or lemon before drying. This can aid in preventing the browning that occurs while drying apples. Simply soak the fruits in the juice of a lemon for 5 minutes, then rinse it off before putting it onto the baking tray.

Some fruits, like plums or Apricots can be prepared in simple solutions made up of one component honey and two portions water. The mixture is heated until the honey dissolve. Allow it to cool before allowing it to allow the sliced fruits to soak overnight prior to drying.

The fruits that naturally have waxy coatings, such as blueberries and grapes, for instance, can benefit from being dipped into boiling water for just a few minutes prior to drying. This can make them much simpler to dry.

A properly dried fruit must not have any dry spots. The fruit is crisp and soft, with leather-like both texture and appearance. Be sure that it's dry and completely dried. Cut a slice into two pieces and then try to squeeze it. If the fruit is still damp it will need to let it dry for longer. After it's cooled it is safe to store the fruit in sterilized jars or bags and store them somewhere that is cool and dark.

It's easy to hydrate fruit by placing the fruit in a bowl of boiling water for half an hour, and they will be ready for make use of. Naturally, you could take the fruit and eat it dried. This makes an amazing snack all on its own!

Canning and bottling is another method to keep your fruit in good condition as well as a method that can last for up to a year, or often longer, is by the process of bottling or canned. This is a fantastic option to handle a big fruit harvest. It's generally preserving your fruit by creating relish, jam, jelly, chutney or even just picking the fruit. This technique is used throughout history to provide the ability to access different kinds of foods throughout winter. It's also an enjoyable activity to play with!

There is a way to preserve virtually all kinds of fruits using these techniques. Many fruits can be used to make jelly and jams. Apples and pear are especially great for chutneys. You are able to pickle every fruit you like.

If you're bottling a fruit, it should remain firm and not too ripe. Clean the fruit, and then prepare the fruit as usual, removing the damaged or bruised areas. The smaller fruits are less likely to require cutting, but bigger ones do, especially as there are some that require pits or stone removal.

If you are looking for fruit such as apricots or peaches, which tend to be difficult to cut, it's best to cook the whole fruit in water that is boiling for a couple of minutes, until the skin becomes out, and then drain, chill and peel off the skin. The pears and apples need to be peeled and sliced prior to being cut.

If the fruit is fresh either pureed, cooked or raw depends the recipe you wish to do with the fruit. The ability to bottle soft fruit (plums or cherries, and the like) by using the "raw-pack" technique. Place the fruits in the jar and fill the jar a third at one time. Each layer is covered with syrup made of sugar, which retains the color and taste of the fruit, and also adds to the taste. It is possible to use juice of the fruit or wine if you want.

Firm and fibrous must be made into syrups of sugar first to make them more palatable to store in Jars. This enhances flavor, and also allows the addition of spices like cinnamon, cloves and many more to the fruits. When you simmer the fruit, you could rub it in lemon juice to prevent it from becoming brown.

When you're making a preserver such as this, be sure that the bottles are sterilized completely prior to putting any fruits into the bottles. Rinse them with hot water. Then, you can place upside down in an oven for a half-hour at 150C. It warms them up to ensure they're hot to fill with liquid.

If you are making the sugar mixture you should use a moderate temperature and a non-metal saucepan. This helps dissolve the sugar properly, and decrease the possibility of burning.

Keep in mind that the mix can shrink after drying and cools. You could need to tap the bottles to get rid of air bubbles that could result in the preserve becoming sloppy.

Close the jars after you've added your mix. If you're using metal lids, it is necessary to cover the lid with greaseproof paper prior to sealing (secure the paper with a rubber band) to stop the mix from corrosion of the metal and altering the flavor.

The best way to preserve your preserves in a cool, dark place. dark as if it's too hot, it can encourage bacteria to multiply. If it's too bright, your preserve's color will diminish.

Chapter 10: Freezing Fruit

Fruit can be frozen, which is an excellent option to preserve fruits during the cold winter months. It is generally faster and less laborious than other ways and allows you to keep a large amount of fruits for use in the future this is particularly useful when you've got a large fruit harvest. It's simple to take it out of the freezer and mix into your personal recipes when you are making food items.

Make sure to freeze the firm fruit which has been picked and is ripe. It requires blanching before freezing it. If you are able to freeze your fruit right after the fruit is harvested you will be able to preserve greater nutrients and flavor. Do not eat any fruit that is damaged or bruised, or take the time to cut them off prior to making the freeze.

It is possible to freeze fruit in ziplock bags made of plastic. It is important to ensure that you put the fruit in a tight container the bag so that you leave less space as possible. Make sure it is properly sealed so that it is not able to let air in. It is a good idea to weigh out every bag, so whenever you go to grab an item that is frozen it is clear how much will receive. This can prevent your from taking a lot of fruits from the freezer, only to think about which to do with the rest.

If you want to preserve fruit like apples, that have a tendency to turn brown, put them in lemon juice prior to taking them to the freezer.

Since fruit is soaked in a great deal of water, the fresh or frozen fruits may have a slight different in texture. Keep in mind that fruit frozen is almost always less firm than the fruit that was not frozen.

In the beginning, by blanching the fruit you can stop this from happening. But any blanching process can alter the quality in the flesh of your fruit. It is important to freeze the fruit as quickly as possible so it won't take time in which it could get damaged during the process of freezing.

Sometime, your frozen fruits will get burned by the freezer, that is the result of an excess amount of moisture within the fruit which you've frozen. Make sure to pack your fruits tightly and seal the bag tightly so that it will not suffer freezing burn.

The majority of frozen fruits remain for between eight and twelve months without difficulty, however the more you blanch them and keep their contents in sugar syrup they'll last for a longer time. Prepare a solution of sugar by dissolving 675g sugar in 1.5l of water that is warm. Naturally, you can increase the amount in case you wish to make larger quantities of sugar syrup.

You can use your frozen fruit as is or even freeze it and then defrost it. The best method for defrosting is placing it into a plastic bag and then allowing it to defrost at the room temperatures. Be aware that this may take a while. The speed of defrosting process by placing the plastic bag in cool water. Use the fruit for eating or cooking the fruit as soon as it is defrosted, and best in the coldest temperature.

Fruit that is frozen can be a fantastic method of keeping fruit in good condition as well as ensuring that you are stocked with "fresh" fruit to use in cooking or baking through the entire all the time. When you have a huge amount of fruit, it is the best way to deal to it, and also reducing the amount of waste.

Common Problems With Fruit Trees

The majority of time you will not be faced with problems when you grow fruit trees. However, sometimes you will run into a challenge or two. In this section we will be able to learn about the more frequent problems could arise while making fruit and ways to deal with the issues. However, as that you water regularly and feed and trim your trees for fruit, there ought to have no problems beginning with.

The most serious issue faced by fruit trees is drainage issues. The reason is that water gets soaked into roots due to the fact that the soil has become too saturated. This is the most frequent scenario in high clay content. It is possible to test your soil's drainage by digging a 2-foot-deep hole and filling it with water and then observing the time it takes the water to evaporate. If it is more than 3 hours to drain, then it is likely that you have an issue with drainage.

It is possible to solve drainage issues through digging well-rotted compost or manure in the soil. This can open up the soil, which will allow the water to drain quicker. Plant the tree in the top of a mound if the water logging has been result of rainfall. This will ensure it can let the rain drain out.

Another risk to your fruit trees is an early frost. Since many fruit trees bloom during the early spring months the late freeze can harm the bloom and keep your trees from producing fruits that season.

It is possible to prevent this from happening by a variety of ways. Plant your trees in a protected area or even against a wall in order so that the tree is protected from frost. It is also possible to plant the trees in an area that's not facing so that the blossoms aren't able to develop as early.

Another option is to drape your tree in fleece when it is at risk of an early frost. The tree will need to be removed of it in the morning to allow the bees access to the flowers, and thus be able to pollinate the tree.

Pests are bound to become a major issue everywhere around the globe. Don't let this cause you to be scared as many can be dealt to and can be encouraged by natural predators to eliminate the insects, or at the very least, ensure they are under control.

Birds are a nuisance in particular for trees like cherry and you must employ netting or some other device to keep birds away.

Aphids can be another issue, especially on the branches and the tips of their buds. The aphids can be removed with a hand or spray, or even attract hoverflies, ladybirds, and lacewings to your yard, all of which consider aphids to be a delicious snack. Aphids are usually identified as infestations when you notice an increase in insects on your trees. If you observe ants running through your trees, odds that there's an infestation of aphids near the bottom on the tree.

Codling moth in winter and apple sawfly could be major problems. If you spot them, make sure to keep the areas infested clean as well as burn the affected fruits as well as leaves.

Red spider mites could also cause problems, but when you spray the plants with water, it can keep them out.

Slugs may be seen at the base of younger trees, however less than on mature trees. It is possible to use pellets for slugs or lure hedgehogs and frogs to your yard and they'll consume them.

Being vigilant will often spot bugs before they become an issue that is serious, and decide on the best way to eliminate these.

The effects of diseases can pose a major concern as they may result in ruining the fruits of your labor or destroying the tree. Be sure to remove the fallen leaves, and trim off infected branches. Don't put them in the compost bin; rather, you can Burn them or throw them into the compost bin.

Make sure to prune your trees in a controlled manner and ensure that you take care to cover any wounds you've cut the branches. Make sure to prune your trees only during dry days and delicate trees like apricots for instance, would prefer pruning during the summer months.

There are several ailments that be harmful to fruit trees, however they're fairly rare and shouldn't stop you from cultivating your own fruit trees. If you cultivate fruit trees within the proper conditions and care for it in a way that is safe, you're unlikely to encounter any issues with illnesses.

Prevention is more than a pound cure So by establishing robust plants and taking care of the plants properly, they'll be better positioned to protect themselves from bugs and diseases. Be sure to purchase the plants from a source, since they're more likely to be healthy.

Feed your plants during the first few months of development, but avoid overfeeding your plants because this will cause the plants to develop the sappy, which can be more vulnerable to attacks by diseases as well as pests.

The weeds will only be an issue if you allow they grow too large. If you put mulch mats in the lower part of the tree, it can assist in keeping the weeds under control and keep the weeds from fighting with the fruit tree's supplies. The mulch mat can be purchased mat, or use an old straw, carpet, compost, or a well-rotted horse manure. If you are regularly trimming the tree's base and make sure that the weeds aren't taking over and choke the trees.

Every tree comes with their own range of insects, and apples are experiencing the greatest problems, as they are among the most frequently planted trees.

If you notice ribbon-like marks over the surfaces of your apple, it could be a sign that there is a sawfly on your apple. If you notice leaves that have holes, you may are suffering from winter moth. If you notice maggots on your apple, this usually suggests that you've got an infestation of codling moth. Aphids that are woolly will leave soft areas in the bark of your tree.

Some of the pests that are present are treated using chemical sprays. However, they're not usually organic. This means that you'll be consuming them as you consume the fruit. These pests can affect the flavor of the fruit as well.

If you encourage natural predators into your backyard and making sure that you take care of your tree and care for it, you'll be able to keep diseases and pests in check. If you notice any indication of disease then you must immediately take away and destroy all fruits leaves, branches and other parts with evidence of infection.

In most cases there is no need to notice any indications of disease however, remember that when pruning, you're opening an injury to the tree, and similar to when you injure yourself, it could make the tree vulnerable to the possibility of infection. Applying one of these "paints" to cover the wounds that the tree has following pruning can help decrease the possibility of infection dramatically.

Fruit trees are an enjoyable experience and if you take care of the trees, they're likely to be robust and strong. The majority of times, you're unlikely to encounter an issue, but at the very least, you have enough information that you are prepared.

Chapter 11: Why Grow Your Own Orchard?

A beautiful orchard can be a stunning and productive addition to any home. The view of trees laden with fruit as well as the smell of flowers and the pleasure of picking your own fresh fruits and vegetables are only a few of the benefits which come from cultivating your orchard on your own. In this article we'll explore the numerous reasons for why creating an orchard on your own is an investment worth it.

1. Enjoy Fresh and Nutritious Food:

One of the best advantages of growing your own fruit trees is the possibility of enjoying freshly prepared and healthy meals. Food items from the supermarket often travel long distances, and can take days or months in storage before reaching your plates. However, if you cultivate your own orchard, you will have instant access to a large range of fresh fruits harvested at the peak of their maturity. It is a way to ensure that you get the fruits with a plethora of flavour and packed with vital nutrients, minerals as well as antioxidants.

2. Health Benefits:

The cultivation of your own orchard can provide many advantages for health. In the first place, it promotes a healthy diet that is rich in fresh fruit. Incorporating fruit into every day meals has been proven to lead to better digestion and lower risk of developing chronic illness, and improved general well-being. Furthermore, gardening is an activity physically demanding which provides physical exercise and helps to increase fitness, cardiovascular health as well as flexibility. The act of spending time outside in the fresh air improves your mental health, lowers anxiety, and enhances spirits.

3. Cost Savings:

A further reason that is compelling to plant an orchard on your own is the chance to earn costs savings. There are some initial costs needed to purchase equipment, trees, and equipment, the long-term advantages outweigh the cost. When your orchard has been established and you are able to enjoy an endless supply of fruit and not have to pay high costs at the supermarket. This is especially beneficial for those who have a large family or consume an enormous quantity of fruits regularly. Furthermore, leftover fruit can be kept by making preserves, freezing or canning. making preserves and jams, which allows you to relish your fruit throughout the year.

4. Environmental Impact:

If you grow your own orchards will positively impact the natural environment.

Commercial agriculture usually requires the use of pesticides herbicides and various other chemicals that could affect the ecology and pollute the water supply. If you decide to grow your own orchard, it is possible to can control the growth methods. Choose organic techniques that minimize the use of pesticides and encourage biodiversity by creating the perfect habitat for beneficial birds and insects. In addition cultivating your own food helps reduce the carbon footprint that comes to the transport and storage of your produce.

5. Educational Opportunities:

An orchard can offer great educational opportunities, specifically those with kids. The children can be taught about the process of life in the plants as well as the importance of pollinators, as well as the significance of soil health and its impact on the growth of plants. It is also a great way to develop important life skills, like responsibility, perseverance and the ability to solve problems. Furthermore, tended to an orchard can help foster a sense of connection to nature. It also helps kids to understand the source of their food and can result in better eating habits as well as an appreciation of the natural world.

Making your own orchards is rewarding and fulfilling that has many benefits. From the pleasure of harvesting your own produce to benefits of health, savings on costs and positive environmental impacts, and opportunities for education and more, orchards have everything for anyone.

Benefits of Growing Fruit Trees

Fruit trees are a source of numerous advantages, making it an investment worth making. Below are a few main advantages of establishing fruit trees:

1. Fresh and nutritious produce Grow yourself fruit trees will allow consumers to eat freshly-picked, delicious and high in nutrients. Contrary to store-bought fruit that could be picked too early and then transported over long distances the fruits you grow at home can be harvested when they are ripe, which means the best taste and nutrition. Fruits are loaded with nutrients, minerals, vitamins as well as antioxidants that help to improve general health and wellbeing.

2. Cost savings In the long time cultivating your own fruit trees could result in significant savings on costs. The prices at the supermarket for fresh fruit can be expensive, especially when they are organically grown. If you cultivate your own trees of fruit, it is no longer necessary to buy expensive fruit frequently. Furthermore, the excess harvest from your trees could be stored by making preserves,

freezing or canning. making preserves and jams, making it possible to enjoy all year long without incurring additional cost.

3. Self-Sufficiency and Food Security The growth of fruit trees can contribute to the self-sufficiency of food and security. The less you rely to food imports and can have more control over the safety and quality of your food. In the event of a food shortage or in times of emergency, an orchard in your backyard can be an important supply of healthy food for your family and you.

4. Environment-friendly Benefits: Trees of fruit have numerous benefits for the environment. The trees absorb carbon dioxide, and expel oxygen, which aids to slow changes in the climate. Additionally, they provide the habitat and nutrients for animals, birds as well as other animals and help to increase the diversity of our ecosystem. In addition, having the fruit trees yourself will allow you to reduce or

even eliminate hazardous pesticides and other chemicals in order to reduce the amount of pollution and protect the natural world.

5. Aesthetics and landscaping: Fruit trees can improve the appearance of your house and contribute to the beauty of your landscape. Fruit trees that blossom in the spring produce a lively and stunning display. mature trees that are laden with fruit provide color and texture your landscape. Fruit trees will also enhance the value of your home, which makes it more attractive to potential buyers in the event that you decide to sell the property in the future.

6. Opportunities for Education: The cultivation of fruit trees provides excellent learning opportunities for kids, especially. Children can be taught about the cycle of life for trees, the significance of pollination and also the significance of insects in

producing fruit. Engaging in hands-on tasks such as cutting, planting and harvesting can help children develop more understanding and appreciation of nature. helping to promote environmental stewardship as well as sustainability practices.

7. Community and sharing A fruit tree can help create a sense of community as well as provide an opportunity for sharing. If you've got a large fruit harvest, it is possible to offer your surplus fruit to your friends and neighbors or food banks in your area which will increase goodwill while reducing the amount of food wasted. Being involved in community orchards, or the planting of fruit trees gives you the opportunity to meet people who share your interests, swap information, and participate in our efforts to encourage the sustainable production of food.

Fruit trees can provide many benefits, that range from delicious and healthy produce, to the savings on costs, environmental benefits and learning opportunities. If you've got a tiny backyard or larger area plant fruit trees could provide a satisfying and rewarding adventure with lasting rewards.

The Joy of Harvesting Your Own Fruit

The process of picking your own fruits can be an enjoyable and fulfilling process. No matter if you've got a modest backyard garden or have access to an orchard that is larger and garden, growing and harvesting your own fruit will bring you closer to the natural world, provide you with fresh delicious produce and provide a sense satisfaction. There are a few reasons picking your own fruits can provide you with joy

1. Connecting With Nature The process of growing your own fruits lets you connect to the world around you in a meaningful manner. Watch the trees grow during spring, watch the fruit develop and mature throughout time before you finally take pleasure in the fruits you harvest. This is a stunning sequence that lets you experience the beauty of nature as well as the seasons that change.

2. Freshness and flavor Freshness and Flavor: Nothing is better than fresh-picked fruits. When you take fruit right off the tree and it's at best ripeness, flavor and savor. The flavor is usually much more intense and vivid compared to the store-bought fruits that could had been picked earlier in order to be able to stand the stress of transportation.

3. Benefits for health Producing your own fruits gives you access to healthy, organic fruits and vegetables. You control the

entire process of growth that allows you to be free of chemical pesticides and other harmful substances. Freshly picked fruits are also high in minerals, vitamins and antioxidants that contribute to healthy eating habits as well as overall health.

4. A sense of accomplishment A sense of accomplishment: Watching a small seed mature into a fruiting tree can be a satisfying moment. If you are able to harvest your own fruits and are proud in the work and effort you invest in nurturing your trees. This is a tangible achievement that will boost confidence levels and provide feelings of satisfaction.

5. Community and Family Engagement Fruit harvesting is an excellent way to engage your loved ones and family as part of a group project. It unites people to encourage teamwork, builds trust, and helps create lasting memories. It is possible to involve kids and educate them

on the world around them as well as the importance in sustainable production of food and the delight in growing your own food.

6. Cost savings: Growing the fruits yourself will help you save money over the long term. Although there might be beginning investments made that include plants, seeds, or garden tools, after your trees begin to grow in the ground, they'll provide an abundance of fruit each year. It can drastically reduce costs for groceries, as well as provide your with top-quality food for a fraction of the price.

7. Sustainable Living: Growing your own fruits is in line with the tenets that sustain living. When you grow your own food, you can reduce the carbon footprint of transport and reduce the requirement for processing and packaging. It's a sustainable option to eat fresh and seasonal fruits and vegetables.

Don't forget that preparing yourself produces time patience, dedication as well as ongoing attention. You'll have to provide the plants with sun, water, and nutrients. You'll also need to guard them against disease and pests. The joy in the process of growing or harvesting own fruits is worth your time and work.

Environmental Benefits of Fruit Tree Cultivation

The cultivation of fruit trees offers a variety of advantages for the environment that help to promote the sustainability of our lives and efforts to conserve. Here are a few important environmental advantages associated with growing fruit trees:

1. Carbon Sequestration: The fruit trees as well as all other trees are essential to carbon sequestration. Through photosynthesis, they take carbon dioxide

(CO2) out of the atmosphere and transform to oxygen and store carbon within their trunks, branches and root. When you plant fruit trees, they can aid in reducing climate change by decreasing the carbon dioxide (CO2) within the atmosphere.

2. Biodiversity support: The fruit trees provide the habitat and the food source to a wide range of species of wildlife including the birds, insects and even small mammals. They attract pollinators, including butterflies and bees. These help in the reproduction of a variety of plant species. In creating an ecosystem that is diverse that includes fruit trees, you can contribute to the conservation and preservation of the biodiversity local to you.

3. Soil Conservation: Fruit trees help prevent soil erosion. The extensive root systems of their roots anchor soil,

decreasing the chance of erosion by runoff from the wind or rain. The leaves of fruits trees are also a natural mulches, enhancing soil fertility and retention of moisture.

4. Conservation of Water: mature fruit trees are rooted deep which can allow for water to flow further in the earth. This means that they do not require extensive irrigation, in particular when as compared to crops that are grown annually. If you grow fruit trees you are able to conserve water as well as encourage a more sustainable consumption.

5. Reducing food miles yourself your own fruits reduces the distance food items must be transported from the farm to your table. It also reduces emission of carbon dioxide from transportation that includes the use of fuel as well as greenhouse gas emission. If you plant fruits trees in your garden You can taste local, fresh products

while also reducing your environmental footprint.

6. Pesticides and Chemical Reduction Pesticide and Chemical Reduction: Commercial production of fruit typically rely upon the use of pesticides, fungicides and other chemical substances to shield the crops from disease and pests. If you grow your own fruits is a chance to choose organic or cultivars that are pesticide-free, thus reducing the emissions of hazardous chemicals to the surrounding environment, and helping to create healthier ecosystems.

7. Preservation of Genetic Diversity: Many classic and heirloom fruit trees are in danger of disappearing because commercial agriculture's emphasis is on a narrow range of yield-producing cultivars. If you plant a wide variety of fruits tree species can contribute to preservation of genetic diversity and conserving unique

tastes as well as textures and strength within the fruit crop.

In general, the cultivation of fruit trees has numerous environmental benefits such as carbon sequestration, habitat conservation, biodiversity as well as water conservation. They also help reduce the number of miles food travel, reductions in pesticides as well as genetic diversity conservation. Incorporating fruit trees into your landscaping, you'll be able to positively impact your environment and enjoy the rewards of your efforts.

Chapter 12: Choosing the Right Fruit Trees

The right choice of fruit trees to plant in your backyard or orchard is an essential step to making sure you get a fruitful harvest. Things like weather, soil conditions availability of space and individual preferences are crucial considerations to consider when picking the right fruit trees. In this article we'll delve more into the different aspects to take into consideration while selecting the right fruit trees.

1. Climate and Hardiness:

One of the main aspects to take into consideration when choosing fruits trees are the weather conditions in the region you are in. Certain fruit trees are suited to specific conditions for temperature and climate to allow maximum growth and production. Certain fruit trees flourish in tropical, warm environments, whereas others tend to thrive in areas with cooler temperatures. Knowing the climate of your area and identifying varieties of fruit trees which are suitable for this will significantly improve your odds of succeeding.

2. Soil Conditions:

A second important aspect to consider is the condition of the soil in the orchard, garden or backyard. The soil of fruit trees has different preferences. It is crucial to choose plants that match the soil you have. The soil's pH, drainage, as well as fertility must be evaluated. A soil test could provide useful information on the content of nutrients in soil and the pH, assisting you to choose the right fruit trees to flourish in the soil.

3. Space and Site Selection:

Space and location choice are important factors that should be considered when picking fruits trees. Certain fruit trees such as apples and pear trees, need a lot of spaces and should be planted in a space with enough space between them in order so that they can grow properly and circulation of air. However certain varieties of fruit trees such as espaliered or dwarf trees, can be adapted to smaller spaces, or are planted against fences or walls. Consider the space you have available and choose the right fruit trees for the area you have chosen.

4. Pollination and Fruit Set:

Certain varieties of fruit trees need cross-pollination in order to grow fruit. It is important to think about what requirements to pollinate the tree you pick. Certain trees self-pollinating that is, they are able to create fruit by themselves however, others need a separate variety near for pollination. Make sure you pick varieties that complement each other or installing multiple trees for that you have the right pollination conditions and fruit set.

5. Disease and Pest Resistance:

Pest and disease resistance must be considered when selecting fruit trees. Certain varieties are more natural resistance to most common illnesses and pests, decreasing the requirement for regular sprays of pesticides, as well as making them simpler to maintain. Find varieties resistant to disease that will be a good fit for the area you live in to reduce risks and boost the likelihood of a profitable harvest.

6. Taste and Harvest Time:

Personal preferences about the taste of fruits and taste and harvest time are a major factor when choosing a fruit tree. The different varieties of fruit have a range of textures, flavors, and harvest time. Be aware of the preferences for taste in the family and pick trees that provide the fruit you love. Also, choosing varieties that have time-stamps that allow for a more regular harvest can prolong your season of fruit bearing and provide an extended time of fun.

Selecting the best fruit trees is a matter of considering a variety of elements like the climate, soil conditions, availability of space, requirements for pollination, resistance to disease, as well as individual preferences in taste. When you carefully consider these aspects and choosing appropriate trees, you can establish a successful orchard or fruit garden that produces tasty fruits in the years to come.

Climate Zones and Hardiness Zones and zones for hardiness play a significant factor in determining the ability of a variety of fruits trees to the specific area. Understanding these zones will help the orchard and garden owners choose types of trees that are able to be able to withstand local climate conditions and flourish in their region. Below is a more thorough description of the zones for hardiness and climate

1. Climate Zones:

Climate zones are regions that are classified by their long-term conditions, such as temperatures, precipitation and seasonal changes. Climate zones provide an understanding of the weather conditions that prevail in an area. They generally defined based on factors like temperature range or the length of the growing season. Common classifications for climate zones comprise subtropical, tropical, temperate and subtropical, temperate and cold zones.

Tropical Climate: Tropical areas typically experience warm to hot temperatures all year round, and with only minor variation in temperature during the season. The regions are characterised by high humidity and a lot of rain. The fruit trees that flourish in tropical climates include mangoes papayas, bananas, and citrus fruit.

Subtropical Climate Subtropical areas have hot to warm summers as well as cool winters that are mild, with a few fluctuations in temperature during the season. They experience moderate rain and levels of humidity. Trees that thrive in subtropical climates are avocados, citrus fruits, figs as well as some kinds of plums and peaches.

Temperate Climate: The regions with temperate climates possess distinct seasons that include mild summers as well as cool winters that are cold to cool. They typically receive regular rainfall all through the all of the year. The most commonly grown fruit trees in climates with temperate temperatures include fruits like cherries, apples, pears Apricots, peaches and plums.

Cold Climates The cold climates experience long cold winters that are cold and generally short growing seasons. They are often prone to frigid temperatures as well as snowfall. Trees that thrive in colder climates include apple, pears, cherry (specific varieties) as well as plums (specific kinds) as well as a few varieties of berries, like currants and raspberries.

2. Hardiness Zones:

Zones of hardiness provide specific details on the temperatures in winter that trees or plants will be able to tolerate. It is the United States Department of Agriculture (USDA) Hardiness Zone Map is used extensively to establish the zones of hardiness in the specific region. The map breaks regions down into zones numbered by number which each one representing an individual temperature range.

As an example the Zone 9 means that the zone has an average winter temperatures between 20 and 30 degree Fahrenheit (-6 to -1 degree Celsius) in comparison to Zone 4. Zone 4 indicates a minimum temperature range of between -30 and 20 degree Fahrenheit (-34 to -29 Celsius). Knowing the zones of hardiness that you live in and the zone of your location, you are able to choose types of fruit trees that will be suitable for the winter temperature of your region.

It is important to remember that although hardiness zones typically are focused on winter temperatures but other elements such as the summer heat, humidity and rain patterns must also be taken into consideration for the cultivation of fruit trees.

Knowing the climate and zones of hardiness is vital to choose varieties of fruit trees that are well-adapted to the climate of your area. If you choose fruit trees which are suited to the zones of hardiness and climate in your area, you can increase your chances of a successful development, production of fruit as well as overall health of the tree.

Selecting Fruit Tree Varieties

In selecting the best fruit tree variety There are a variety of things to be considered to ensure that you select the best tree for your requirements and the growing environment. Below are some key points to remember:

1. The climate suitability of different fruit trees require a specific climate. Be aware of your local climate which includes temperature variations such as frost dates, afghans, as well as chilling times (the

amount of time under a particular temperature for the fruit to develop). Pick varieties that will be best suited to the climate you live in.

2. Space availability: Think about the amount of space you have in your backyard or orchard. Certain fruit trees need greater space than other varieties. Be sure to check the maturity size of the tree, and make sure that you have the space needed for it to expand and spread easily.

3. The requirements for pollination: Certain fruit trees can self-pollinate, that is, they are able to grow fruit by themselves. Other varieties require cross-pollination. two varieties that are compatible are required for fruit sets that are successful. If cross-pollinating is required make sure you have the space to accommodate multiple trees, or opt for self-fertile ones.

4. Resistance to disease: Study the most common pests and diseases that affect fruits trees in your local area. Find varieties with the ability to resist or even tolerate the problems. These varieties are more resistant to diseases and can help you save time and effort when it comes to managing the pests and illnesses.

5. Harvest time Time of harvest: Fruit trees have various harvest times. Think about when you would like to pick and relish the fruit, and pick varieties that mature at the right time. So, you'll be able to prepare for an ongoing harvest of fresh fruit all through the year.

6. Taste and the intended purpose Be aware of your personal preferences as well as the purpose for which you intend to use the fruit. Certain varieties are best for eating fresh, whereas others can be used for baking, cooking or even canning. Review descriptions and read reviews to

gain an understanding of the taste and texture of the fruits.

7. Local suggestions: Talk to local nursery companies, agricultural extension offices or knowledgeable gardeners in the area you live in. They will provide important information about the top fruit trees that are thriving in your local area.

When you take into consideration these aspects when choosing a the varieties of fruit trees that are appropriate for your area, climate as well as your personal tastes, which will ensure the best and most abundant harvest.

Considerations for Small Spaces

If you're limited on spaces in your backyard or you wish to plant fruit trees in containers for your terrace or balcony, there are several additional things to take into consideration:

1. Varieties with a semi-dwarf or dwarf appearance Find trees that have been specifically designed to be smaller, mature size. The dwarf or semi-dwarf varieties take smaller spaces and can be more easily cultivated when planted in containers or small spaces. They are able to be pruned and trained to be small while still yielding an abundance of fruit.

2. Espalier or trellis training Espalier is a process where trees are taught to spread flat against walls or trellis employing horizontal supports as well as careful pruning. This lets you grow fruits vertically, thereby conserving space, as well as creating a beautiful aspect. Certain varieties of trees like apples and pear trees, are suited to training in the espalier manner.

3. Pot suitability In the event that you intend to plant fruit trees in containers, be sure your selection of varieties is

appropriate for gardening in containers. Find trees with an elongated root system as well as the ability to thrive in containers. Pick containers that are big enough to hold the tree's roots as well as provide an adequate drainage.

4. Pollination concerns: When you live in tiny spaces, it could be difficult to house several fruit trees to cross-pollinate. Consider self-pollinating varieties, or think about planting multi-grafted trees with multiple varieties compatible within a single tree making sure that cross-pollination is possible within the smallest size.

5. Maintenance and pruning Maintenance and pruning are essential to control the dimensions and shapes of your trees, especially in smaller areas. Find varieties that react easily to pruning and can be maintained in a compact manner. Think about your amount of time and energy

you're willing to put into maintaining your tree when you are choosing the right types.

6. Size and yield of the fruit The size and yield of some varieties of fruits naturally yield smaller-sized fruits that are more appropriate for smaller spaces. Take into consideration the anticipated yield and dimensions of the fruits of the species that you're interested in to determine if they meet the space restrictions and consumption demands.

Make sure you provide enough sunshine, water as well as nutrients to your trees of fruit no matter the dimensions of your gardening area. If you take care of them and select a variety of appropriate types, you can reap the advantages of growing your own fruit even in smaller garden spaces or in containers.

Chapter 13: Orchard Planning and Design

Orchards are meticulously planned and designed areas that are planted with fruit bearing trees to serve a variety of purposes, whether personal or commercial. Design and planning of an orchard plays a crucial part in the long-term viability in terms of productivity, sustainability, and efficiency. In this article we'll explore the most important factors and the steps that are that are involved in designing and planning, which includes the selection of the site, trees spacing, layout irrigation and pest control. If you follow these rules and guidelines, owners of orchards can develop productive and sustainable orchards.

Selecting the Ideal Site

The selection of the ideal location for your orchard is the beginning step for orchard planning and design. The characteristics of the site will greatly affect the long-term viability of your orchard as well as its productivity. Below are the most important factors to take into consideration when choosing an optimal site for your orchard

1. Soil Qualities: The soil's quality that is present on the property is crucial because it affects tree's nutrient content and general well-being. Perform a thorough analysis of the soil to evaluate its fertility, texture drainage, and pH. Certain fruit trees need specific soil conditions So, choose a location which has a soil that's healthy, well-drained and rich in organic matter and suitable for the chosen species of fruit trees.

2. Climate: The weather of the location is a major factor in determining which fruit tree species that will flourish in the region. Be aware of factors like the temperature range, frost incidence along with chilling hours as well as annual rainfall. Each fruit

has its own requirements for their climates, so pick an area where the climate corresponds to the demands of the particular fruit plant species you want to plant.

3. The availability of water: Proper access to water is crucial for the growth and establishment in the growth of fruits trees. Examine the water source of your site as well as access to irrigation sources for water as well as the reliability of rainfall that is natural. In the case of the location it is possible think about supplementary irrigation strategies for ensuring a constant flow of water during dry times.

4. Sunlight Exposure: Trees that produce fruit need adequate sunlight to photosynthesis and production of fruit. Examine the location's exposure to sun all day long and throughout the all year. Be sure that the area gets full sun, or at least the minimal amount of sunshine required

for the selected fruit tree. Beware of sites that have excessive shade due to trees, buildings or other structures that hinder sunlight's penetration.

5. Topography. It is the topography the area affects water drainage, air flow as well as the possibility of frost pockets. Select a location with the slightest slope in order to allow the proper drainage of water and avoid the accumulation of water. Consider the area's exposure to current wind and frost-prone zones. Avoid areas with low elevations where the cold air could build up and cause damage to frost on the trees.

6. Accessibility: Take into consideration the ease of access to the area to transport and administration activities. An easy access to the orchard can facilitate the transportation of equipment, machinery and the harvested fruit. An adequate road infrastructure as well as close proximity to

markets should be considered in particular for commercial orchards.

7. Pests and diseases: Examine your site for signs of problems with pests and diseases. Avoid areas where there is the history of significant disease or pests that could adversely affect the health of the orchard. Close proximity to other orchards or hosts that are susceptible to disease should be considered in order to lower the chance of pest or diseases transmission.

8. Considerations for the Environment Be aware of any restrictions or environmental laws or conservation measures within the region. Be aware of the effects that the orchard's impact on the surrounding ecosystem, which includes habitats for wildlife as well as water bodies and protected zones. Following sustainable agricultural methods and minimizing the environmental impact must be the top concern.

If you take care to consider these elements when choosing a site By carefully considering these factors, you will be able to select the optimal location for your orchard, which will provide favorable growth conditions, improves productivity as well as ensures sustainability for the long term.

Soil Preparation and Testing

Testing and preparation of soil is a crucial step when planning and designing of orchards. The performance of an orchard heavily depends on the quality and health of the soil since it is directly affecting the development, development, and productivity of the fruit trees. A proper soil preparation and testing will ensure that soil is in the best condition for the orchard, which allows the trees to flourish and grow high-quality fruits. This is a comprehensive description of soil preparation and testing for orchard designing and planning:

Soil Preparation:

1. Soil Analysis: The initial step to prepare soil is conducting a thorough soil analysis. The process involves collecting soil samples from various places within the orchard and transferring samples to a lab to be tested. This analysis will provide information on the content of nutrients in soil and pH levels as well as the organic matter content and the texture. These data help identify the soil amendments and fertilizers needed to enhance the quality of soil and to correct any deficiencies.

2. Soil Amendments: Based upon the results of soil analyses soil amendments could be required to improve the conditions of the soil for development of the fruit tree. The most common

amendments are lime to regulate the pH of soil organic matter, such as manure or compost to enhance fertility and structure of the soil and specialized nutrients such as nitrogen, phosphorus, or potassium, based on the deficiencies found during the soil analysis. These amendments are usually integrated into the soil prior to planting to allow the soil to be thoroughly mixed and provide benefits to the new trees.

3. Drainage of Soil A proper drainage system is vital to the health of your orchard, since excess water or poor drainage of soil may result in root rot, and various other issues. If your orchard has issues with drainage, it might be necessary to set up drainage structures like tiles drains or French drains so that the any excess water is effectively eliminated. Alternately, raised beds or mounds are a

possibility for drainage improvement when the soil is in poor conditions.

4. Soil Tillage: Based on the soil's condition as well as the requirements specific to fruits, soil tillage could be needed. Tillage can help break down compacted soil, enhances the aeration process, and aids in roots' access. But, overor under-utilized cultivation can cause soil erosion and lower the organic matter content. It is essential to find the right balance, and to follow suggested practices for tillage based on the nature of the soil and trees.

Soil Testing:

1. Nutrient Analyses: Regular soil tests assists in monitoring the level of nutrients within the soil of the orchard and gives insight into need for fertilizer to the trees. Analysis of nutrients helps to identify the right kind and amount of fertilizers needed to ensure an optimal level of nutrient for

good development of the tree and production of fruit. Testing of soil should be conducted at the beginning of each growing season in order to alter fertilizer programs according to the season.

2. Tests for pH: Soil pH is directly related to the availability of nutrients for the plants. Fruit trees have distinct pH needs and soil tests help identify the pH levels of the soil in an orchard. In the event that pH levels are either too excessive (alkaline) or is too low (acidic) amending substances like sulfur or lime are able to be added in order to alter the pH back to the preferred levels for maximum tree growth.

3. Soil Texture: The texture of the soil refers to the ratio of silt, sand, and clay particles, affects the capacity of water to hold, drainage and even root development. Tests on soil help determine the texture of soil, which allows orchardists make educated decision-

making regarding irrigation techniques or drainage improvement, as well as soil amendments.

4. Pest and Disease Testing: Pest Testing and Pest Testing: In addition to testing pH and nutrient levels soil tests can assist in identifying pathogens that cause disease or pests within the soil in an orchard. This is crucial in implementing the right disease management methods and identifying pest-resistant varieties. Tests on soil can reveal any nematodes fungal pathogens, and other hazardous organisms which could impact the health of trees and their productivity.

5. Regular Monitoring: Testing of the soil must be done regularly to observe fluctuations in the soil's fertility, pH, as well as other variables throughout time. It allows for orchardists adapt the management of their soil practices to

guarantee the long-term performance and health of their orchard.

Testing and preparation of soil are essential to the planning and design of an orchard. Through conducting soil analyses and implementing the necessary amendments to improve drainage in the soil and conducting routine tests on soil, orchardists can provide the best conditions for fruit trees to grow. This will ensure healthy growth as well as high-quality fruit and the best productivity for the orchard. The proper preparation of soil and the testing are crucial investments that add to the longevity of the orchard operation.